The Punch Book of Inflation

THE
PUNCH
BOOK
OF
INFLATION

Edited by WILLIAM DAVIS

DAVID & CHARLES
In Association with Punch
NEWTON ABBOT   LONDON   NORTH POMFRET (VT)   VANCOUVER

Printed in Great Britain by
The Leagrave Press Ltd., Luton and London for Punch Publications and
David & Charles (Holdings) Limited   South Devon House   Newton Abbot
Devon.
Published in the United States of America by
David & Charles Inc North Pomfret Vermont 05053 USA
Published in Canada by
Douglas David & Charles Limited 3645   132 Philip Avenue   Vancouver BC

CONTENTS

"Krugerrands!"

Introduction

THERE is a story about a man who decided to have himself frozen until, at some future date, scientists found a cure for his ailment. Before he did so, he called his stockbroker and asked to have all his money put into future growth situations. Time passed, a cure was found, and he had himself defrosted. One of his first acts was to phone the broker's office.

"Tell me," he said, "how have my stocks done over the past sixty years?"

"Oh yes," said the voice at the other end. "My grandfather told me about you. One moment, while I check . . . well, they've had their ups and downs, you know, booms, slumps, war, peace, but your account is now worth just over £3,000,000."

"That's marvellous," he said. "No more money worries—I can really enjoy living again."

At this point the operator cut in: "That will be £30,000 for the next three minutes please."

For anyone who experienced Germany's hyper-inflation of the twenties that is a decidedly sick joke. Even in Britain it doesn't sound so funny any more. Inflation—the equivalent, someone once said, of looking at your savings through the wrong end of a telescope—has proved a deadly foe. And efforts to "hedge" against it have frequently turned out to be costly and embarrassing flops.

This book takes a light-hearted look at what Fleet Street has dubbed "the scourge of the century". I have included cartoons from the distant past to show that inflation, as such, is not new. You will also find *Punch* writers and cartoonists offering their own tongue-in-cheek solutions. Inevitably the emphasis is on self-protection and, of course, a key feature of this is the Anti-Money Game.

The basic rules of the Game are simple. One, don't hold onto money—spend it. You can put £100,000 into a bank vault, have it watched by armed guards twenty-four hours a day, and go in every morning to count it. The £100,000 will still be there at the end of the year—*but* inflation will have robbed you of £20,000. Two, borrow as much as you can and invest it in good antique furniture, property, or Krugerrands. They may well show you a useful capital gain, and of course repayment is in devalued currency.

Carried to extremes, inflation leads to the breakdown of the whole money-exchange system. In early post-war Germany (and, to a lesser extent, in Britain) barter more or less replaced coins and bits of paper. People were broke with lots of money in their pockets. Bicycle tubes, tyres, chocolate bars, cigarettes, tins of sardines—they were the generally accepted mediums of exchange. I happened to be there at the time and I well remember the reverence in which I—a young boy—held luxuries like chocolate and sardines. It never occurred to me that they had originally been made for eating: in my eyes, they were money. We have obviously not reached anything like that stage, but there are people who have stocked up on sardines and baked beans because they think it's only a matter of time before history repeats itself.

The Game, of course, isn't much use if, like most people, you don't have the funds to play it. You can't get much of an overdraft if your income is £30 a week, and you can certainly forget about costly antiques and £70,000 homes. Rushing into cocoa, tin, German Marks, Louis XV commodes and Picasso paintings isn't easy if you live in Coronation Terrace, Edgbaston. But even those with ample means have run into problems.

City Editors used to argue that equities were the best hedge against inflation: pick a "good share" and you couldn't go wrong. No one has the nerve to claim that now. There are too many bewildered small investors who have reason to know better.

Some of the other "hedges" fashionable just a few years ago have proved equally disappointing. Prices of commodities like cotton, copper, zinc and tin, for example, have been hit by the worldwide business recession. In Devon and Cornwall, people are selling hotels

"My God, Russell, you're not trying to forget inflation on the '64 Mouton Rothschild?"

*"You just can't get it into their thick heads that it costs **twice** as much these days to avoid eternal damnation!"*

at knock-down prices rather than face another season. And even the art market is no longer a Sure Thing. Ask the people who stocked up on Dutch romantic landscapes and cheerfully took them along to an auction at Christie's. Most remained unsold: if it hadn't been for a kindly Arab with "eclectic tastes" the whole affair would have been gloomier still. Nothing seems safe—not even Swiss Banks, as Harold Wilson could tell you if he wasn't so busy keeping a low profile.

Dealers have a nice line in sales talk, including generous references to inflation and financial crisis, but they have been known to tell a different story when you try to sell the stuff: suddenly, the market has become "difficult". A favourite trick is to corner the market in, say, Victorian chamberpots and Edwardian porcelain geese and persuade a few trendy journalists to write about it. Some people will buy anything—however hideous and useless— if you can convince them that it makes a good investment. I once went to a dinner party given by a wealthy property developer who owned a fine collection of Lowrys. A fellow guest, one of the richest men in Britain, had never heard of Lowry before and didn't like his paintings. They reminded him too much of his humble origins. But he showed great interest when I told him how much their value had risen in the past decade. Indeed, he talked about nothing else for the rest of the evening, and I believe he is now the hopeful owner of several Lowrys himself. He still doesn't like them, but his guests are impressed. They not only confirm that he is wealthy, but are seen as proof that he has shrewd judgement.

There are people who collect old medicine bottles, empty hand grenades, rusty keys, porcelain parasol handles, historic corkscrews, and Victorian chimney-pots. There are others who, apparently, think nothing of paying £116,000 for a one-cent British Guinea Magenta stamp of 1856. There are people who will urge you to invest in books (someone paid £400 for *Histoire Naturelle des Poissons du Bassin du Leman* at Sotheby's the other day) and people who put their faith in Victorian sheet music and first issues of magazines like

9

*"What this damn country needs is some **creative** inflation."*

Punch and *Playboy*. Old comics have done well in America: issues of *Batman, Superman, The Detective* and *Plastic Man* from the late 1930s and early 1940s can bring as much as 150 dollars. There is also a useful market in autographs; Abe Lincoln would be amazed to hear that a hastily scribbled note ("I was coming down this afternoon, but if you prefer I should not, I shall blame you if you do not tell me so") now sells at $1,500. Not least, it is still possible to make money by backing talented young painters.

Fashion, however, plays havoc even with the more expensive and worthwhile collector's items—witness those landscapes. And postage stamps, books, comics, paintings and coins won't feed you if we really run into trouble. Humphrey Lyttelton says the best bet is to turn yourself into an entertainer. They always do well in bad times. Rudy Vallee, "who played the saxophone and sang sloppy songs into a megaphone," earned $7,500 a week through the Great Depression. A Texas store last Christmas offered lessons in guitar-playing from Jose Feliciano (one full day for a mere £5,600) and in dancing from Mitzi Gaynor (£4,240). If that strikes you as a bit steep, you could at least try to pick up a good second-hand ukulele.

You might also consider Paul Getty's view that depressions are periods of great opportunity. He recalls buying the Hotel Pierre, on New York's Fifth Avenue, for a very modest price at a time when "the gloom-and-doom chaps were too busy titillating their masochistic streaks with pessimistic predictions of worse times to come to recognise such bargains as this when they saw them." The non-conformist who follows his own counsel, he argues, often reaps "fantastic rewards". I dare say that kind of talk sounds a trifle unconvincing to, say, a sheet metal worker in Pittsburgh or a brush salesman in Glasgow. But it would certainly meet with approval from young British tycoons like Jim Slater. He, too, is waiting to pick up the pieces on Doomsday.

But we are not all in the Slater or Getty class. Many people feel the answer to inflation and its attendant problems lies, very simply, in learning to make do with less. People in Western industrial countries, so the argument runs, have been spoiled by prosperity. Depression is "a necessary cultural reorientation". Who needs a second car? Who needs holidays abroad, expensive restaurants, a bigger home? In America, where this kind of talk has been heard for some time, the White House is constantly urging people to make lists of possible savings. When Richard Nixon was President he ate left-overs and turned down his air-conditioner "to set an example". Senior administration officials, not to be outdone, pointed an accusing finger at Mr. and Mrs. America—for driving when they might walk or cycle, for loading the family car up with gadgets that reduced its gasoline efficiency, for buying bigger appliances than they really need, for running the dishwasher and the clothes drier with only half a load, for using self-cleaning ovens instead of elbow grease, for burning unnecessarily bright light bulbs. Gerald Ford has gone in for much the same tactic. Soon after taking over he got his staff to produce WIN buttons (Whip Inflation Now) and, a few days later, called reporters to the Oval Office to read out a letter sent to him by a group of Michigan schoolboys. They promised that, in future, they would turn off all the lights when they were not using them, ride their bikes instead of using Dad's car, always close the door in cold weather, get things out of the refrigerator quickly, and "eat dinner when Mom cooks it so that she will not have to reheat it". Newspapers, too, have urged readers to "be tough with yourself".

It is, of course, easier to sneer at the Gross National Product from a four-bedroom house

"It's a two-hour montage of price tags—it will drive them mad with nostalgia!"

"Well, I suppose it's worth a try."

in the better suburbs of Washington (or, for that matter, Hampstead) than it is from a Baltimore slum. Millions of people have yet to make it to first base. And there is no evidence that newspaper executives are willing to set a good example: it is so much easier to write about these things than to do it yourself. Sacrifices are best made by the other fellow. But we shall all hear more of this kind of advice. The British Government last winter launched a "Keep Britain Cosy" campaign. One suggestion was that everyone should draw all their curtains at night to keep in as much heat as possible; another, from a 24-year old female member of the Government's advisory Council, was that young married couples could save heating "by going to bed and keeping warm in the best way I know".

Inflation is hard on many people—especially those living on fixed incomes—and one should never under-rate its potentially destructive force. But people who talk of impending doom might, perhaps, reflect on this paragraph which recently appeared in the *Chicago Tribune*:

"Look around you, baby. You think we've got troubles. Try a Honduran hurricane for size. They ran out of gasoline to bury the bodies of the dead. Or how about a South American plague? Or starving people and cattle in Africa? Or the lack of basic freedoms and human dignity behind the Iron Curtain?"

Amen.

William Davis

PART 1
THE GOLDEN
AGE
OF INFLATION

THE MAN WHO MENTIONED THE CRISIS AT A COCKTAIL PARTY.

SO VERY NATURAL.

Banker. "I wish you a Happy and Prosperous New Year."
Smart Broker. "Thanks, that depends entirely on *you*, Sir."

THE MENACE OF MAY.

Austen Chambermaid (to John Bull). "YOUR TEA AND THE MORNING PAPER, SIR."

FINANCE.

Grocer. "What's for you, Missy?"

Missy. "Farden's worf o' Soda, Farden's worf o' Soft Soap, Farden's worf o' Treacle, Farden Packet o' Tacks, Farden's worf o' Butter-scrapin's Farden's worf o' Starch, Farden's worf o' Bull's-eyes, an' a Farden Dip."

Grocer. "That'll be Twopence, please."

Missy. "An' what'll be the Discount for Cash?"

THE WAR AGAINST THE PUBLIC.

Profiteering Hen. "NOTHING DOING AT FIVEPENCE. BUT I MIGHT PERHAPS LAY YOU ONE FOR NINEPENCE. WHAT! YOU THOUGHT THE WAR WAS OVER? NOT *MY* WAR."

A PRICELESS POSSESSION.

Mrs. Golightly. "OH, I HOPE YOU WON'T THINK IT RUDE, BUT WOULD YOU MIND TELLING ME WHAT THAT WONDERFUL BLACK STONE YOU'RE WEARING IS?"

Mrs. Lucor. "OH, CERTAINLY. I FIND MOST PEOPLE ENVY ME THAT. IT'S A PIECE OF REAL ENGLISH COAL!"

Mrs. Golightly. "HOW WONDERFUL! AH, I WISH MY HUSBAND WAS A MILLIONAIRE!"

18

Milliner. "THAT MODEL IS FIFTEEN GUINEAS, MODOM."   *Customer.* "HOW MUCH WOULD IT BE IF THE FEATHER WERE REMOVED?"
Milliner. "FIFTEEN-AND-A-HALF GUINEAS, MODOM. YOU SEE, LABOUR IS SO DEAR."

"I suppose your landlord asks a lot for the rent of this place?"
"A lot! He asks me for it nearly every week."

A CONTENTED MIND.

Angelina. "INCOMES UNDER £150 A YEAR ARE EXEMPT FROM INCOME-TAX.
ISN'T IT LUCKY, DARLING? WE JUST MISS IT BY FIVE POUNDS!"

PAYMENT IN KIND.

WHAT THE FALL FROM THE GOLD STANDARD MIGHT BRING US TO.

"A COUPLE OF STALLS, PLEASE."

"THE EVENING PAPER, PLEASE."

"SIX CABINET PHOTOGRAPHS, PLEASE."

"A COLLAR-STUD, PLEASE."

MINOR POET SETTLES HIS BILL AT
A RESTAURANT—

AND LEAVES A TRIFLE UNDER THE PLATE
FOR THE WAITER.

"IN SETTLEMENT OF MY TAX ARREARS."

"RUINED, ALBERT? AND SHALL WE HAVE TO LEAVE OUR LITTLE NEST?"

"Have you noticed any signs yet that people are economising?"
"Oh, yes, Madam. Even the people who never paid don't buy anything now."

Clerk. "As I'm getting married, Sir, is there any chance of an increase in salary?"

Principal. "If you don't get out of here quick we'll make you a partner and you won't get anything."

Fougasse

"No, I don't think we ought to go out anywhere with this crisis going on—and with this crisis going on we probably shan't get in anywhere."

Ah, the great days when we threw away the poker!

by E. S. TURNER

Don't waste fuel
On a vegetabuel!
It's more to your credit
To shred it.

THAT WAS A Government Poem at the darkest hour of World War Two, the hour when a well-known back-bench knight sought to have Churchill replaced by the Duke of Gloucester. Government poems are often a sign that things are not going too well. Heaven knows what might have happened if the nation, by then, had not been united, purified and uplifted by shortages.

You should have seen how we kept the home fires burning. We did it by filling half the fire space with bricks and the rest with green wood and wet slack. We then resolutely shut the damper and *threw away the poker*. But even throwing away that wicked implement was not enough. "Make your fire do the work of several by sharing your fireside with friends," urged the Ministry of Fuel and Power. So we had the Joneses in and smoked their cigarettes, saving valuable timber by sharing their matches ("take a light from a friend"). We then gave them nettle soup. We knew they would have preferred tinned soup, but as Heinz themselves said, "It's worth putting up with no Heinz when millions of Heinz self-heating soup tins are bringing goodness and comfort to our men."

It was more usual to say "our indomitable men". Our indomitable men needed all available film to photograph bomb strikes. They needed all the sparking plugs to maintain the bomber's mighty heart-beat. They needed all the furniture to replace what the officers smashed on mess nights. They also needed every ping-pong ball. Some of us found the scarcity of ping-pong balls intolerable and couldn't wait to join up.

Sometimes the behaviour of our indomitable men united the home front in honest indignation, as when they read of Army swill containing scores of loaves, legs of lamb and even plates and knives and forks. But indignation is just as good a unifier as pride.

It's not easy to keep going when worry floods your stomach with acid and you are miserable with wind and nausea. That's what the Milk of Magnesia people used to say. We were grateful for their help and also for the boundless supplies of aspirin, which gave us "Faith! Hope! Confidence! In Times of Stress!" We needed all our faith and confidence when the Government brought in Macon, which people nowadays think of as plonk. Macon was mutton bacon, just like pork bacon but with no taste. Almost overnight it united the nation against Chamberlain and Hitler, in that order.

When meat rationing came in we all went mad over unrationed offal. Most of us had thought of offal as akin to garbage, but it turned out to mean liver, kidneys, heart and sweetbreads, all the titbits which found their way into the restaurants. You could always get a few scraps of offal, however, by being abnormally civil to your butcher. That was the great thing about shortages—men and women began to make new and often improbable friendships. It was a great help if you were on good terms with the working classes. Many of them weren't used to eating butter and in any event couldn't afford their ration, so they were glad to pass it on for a consideration to the gently nurtured. You wouldn't catch them doing that now. There just isn't the respect any more.

Rich people were thought to be eating unrationed swans and lampreys, and that was something else that linked the nation against a common foe. With a patriotic masochism housewives got down to Ministry of Food hints like "Here is a new notion for using the sweetness of beetroot to make a nice sweet pudding with very little sugar."

There were no sugar cakes in the shops (Robert Boothby, of all people, had seen to that) but if you hoarded some sugar, a very wicked thing to do, you could make a wedding cake of sorts. Yes, there were no bananas for the children; however, as they knew no better you could fob them off with parsnip mashed up with artificial banana flavouring. Cadbury's were always crying, " Please keep milk chocolate for the children," but in the Army you saw brigadiers eating it. Chivers had a heart-warming advertisement in which Jennifer exclaimed to a young brother, "Peacetime parties were wizard, Johnny!" and then tried to tell him what jellies were like, which is harder than it sounds. Johnny couldn't go into the corner shop and ask for his favourite fizzy drink, since all branded soft drinks were discontinued.

Don't think that life for the housewife lacked surprises. The local shop might have a bin of cut-price unlabelled tins, described as "Shipwrecked Stock" (if you were lucky, you could pick up Spam on the beach at Bootle). The trouble with unlabelled tins was that you never knew whether they contained peaches or meat loaf, but it was fun finding out.

And the queues! Men and women alike joined them not knowing what they might find at the end, and exchanged badinage and gossip. They say that one woman, on being informed that the goods offered were for pregnant women only, said, "Keep my place. I'll be back in twenty minutes." How could a nation like that ever be defeated?

Nobody was supposed to ask for second helpings. Restaurants were instructed not to offer bread unless people asked for it (Potato Pete was always nagging us to eat potato bread). The nutritionists say war-time diet did us nothing but good, but what really did us good was going short. When Sir Stafford Cripps, that great good man, got his chance he allowed people only one main course at a restaurant: meat, *or* fish, *or* game, *or* poultry. Best stroke of all, the price of a restaurant meal was limited to five shillings, a sum which today scarcely buys a spoonful of chips.

Clothes rationing was a great boon too. It stopped all ostentation. Nobody was allowed to have pleats, flaps, yokes, capes, flounces, turn-ups, patch pockets or bellows pockets. For some reason there was quite a stir when pockets on pyjama jackets were banned. The dissolute modern generation will say we could have saved millions of yards of cloth by not wearing pyjamas at all, but they have never had to get up in the night to sit with bank managers in shelters.

Many shops managed to hold Fur Weeks during the war. Women were badgered to buy expensive clothes, on the grounds that quality material would cost fewer coupons in the end. The firm of Braemar started a stitch-in-time service; women who sent them frayed undergarments received them back as good as new. As for men, they dug out their old frayed collars and nagged their wives into sewing brown leather patches on their jacket elbows, as if they were dukes. A certain shabbiness was esteemed a virtue, but we were never so aggressively scruffy as a theatre audience today.

Cigarettes were often scarce, and in pursuit of them men made new and beautiful friendships. Advertisers of some commodities would urge the public to go easy with the product, but the tobacco firms never suggested that smoking fewer cigarettes would save seamen's lives. They did say, however: "It is now more than ever necessary to empty your packet at the time of purchase and leave it at your tobacconist's." Mention of paper-saving reminds me that we did not use a new envelope every time we wrote a letter. We sought out a grubby old one and pasted a slip over it, in Inland Revenue fashion. Some people exchanged the same Christmas card, in the same envelope, year after year, showing a rare war-winning spirit.

Those who drove cars drove them at a crawl, to save rubber. At first there was pleasure motoring of a sort. If the ration ran out there was nothing to stop anybody hiring a chauffeur-driven car. Eventually the sight of cars at golf clubs impelled Cripps to put a stop to pleasure motoring. What a glorious mean cheer we gave when Ivor Novello was jailed for fiddling petrol for his Rolls!

If rationing had stopped abruptly after the war the withdrawal symptoms—or do I mean the withdrawal of withdrawal symptoms?—would have been terrible. A sudden wallowing in deep hot baths would have done the national fibre no good; Thank goodness we still had to make do with nutty slack and Utility wardrobes. Thank goodness the brigadiers weren't able to stuff themselves with unlimited milk chocolate.

PART 2
LIVING
WITH
INFLATION

"You beggars are all the same—all you ever think about is money."

"Oh my God! . . . The Acacia Avenue
Prices and Incomes Board!"

"I'm comparison shopping—can you hold the price
of your beans for about half an hour?"

"The chopped sirloin is not for sale. It's a demonstration model."

"Is there a 'Which?' guide to panic buying?"

33

"Only ten minutes until the next price increases, ladies!"

"I keep getting this wave of nostalgia for last week's prices."

"Golly, I'm glad you noticed! There's no point in suffering from depression if nobody notices."

"I hate to keep raising the prices each week but they've come to expect it."

35

THE COLLECTOR

**Living with inflation means living on credit.
According to the debt-collecting agencies, it also means
that they have to get tougher every day . . .**

I get the job

THE pick-up was out on the East Side. 88 Sycamore Terrace was not one of your Campari-belt desirables full of socio-economic oncers a little behind on their backgammon debts or missed a payment on the Three Thousand Five, but it'll come. We're only a small outfit but the debt-collecting business has changed a lot already. It's not a week since we operated three floors up over Holborn Viaduct, writing the clients that an early settlement would oblige, telling them that we'd be putting the matter in the hands of solicitors if a remittance was not received, all of it gentlemanly stuff. We never kicked a door in, once. The clients have been having it soft. The way things are moving now, I give it a month before we get places to cover that'll make us wonder if the bubble-brain running a computer trace from the Home Addresses Bureau has punched in Nelson Rockefeller by mistake, the kind of set-up where the biggest problem will be deciding whether to take the time to go touring up the driveway before the hire-purchase agreement expires. One word with the staff, they'll pay out. This one was different—a two-up, two-down bijou in a street with plenty of cover and a back exit down the alleyway. The card said they had a fridge inside there somewhere. Today, you get seven days behind on a quality appliance like that, it isn't right. We don't like it, that's all. I knew I had to go in, and go in hard.

On my own

MY name is Philip Marlowe. You'd have met me a fortnight back, it'd have been Norman Alsford but, same as I say, the business is changing and I'm changing with it. I'm a collector, self-employed, on contract. Also, I have trouble with my feet. It's my job to be persuasive, with the personal touch. People who lend out cash or give you durables on credit, by and large they're reasonable men. You've made an agreement, they still do polite reminders should you forget. The letters still go out, later on with scarlet stickers on. You choose to ignore them, from now on we get to meet. Reason I mentioned my bad feet earlier on, it could be I get one of them in the door and you push the thing shut, maybe imagine I'm selling brushes or a ten-part History of Bangkok. That I don't like, it is not nice. Often there might be no reason if I've come to re-possess the TV I should re-possess the furniture or take the walls along besides. But I get irritable, you can't tell. So it helps to mention these things, to stay loose and nice and easy. Thought I'd mention it, that's all.

I go in

DON'T mix me up with the milkman, that's another thing. I'm impervious to housewives, suburban or not. I get one opens the door and looks like a Gina Lollobrigida remake, there's no place for feelings. Like this time out I had a yard and a half of top-quality femininity. If this was the lady of the house, I should make a note to advise Ann-Margret to go into real estate; the good days were over. Until this moment, I hadn't known they do chiffon out of aerosol cans. She even still had the sales ticket fastened on a shoulder-strap; the tough ones always spell it out. I flashed her some identity.

"Marlowe," I said. "I collect on the Bendices—washing-machines, driers, refrigerators, all kinds. Friends of mine tell me you're overdue. Probably I'm expected."

"Pardon?" says the housewife. "Is it the rent?" This I get used to. I flicked a Mucron and then set fire to a three-inch mentholated job. The lady throws me one of those smiles you can usually only buy against good collateral. Any minute now, I could expect to have the street full of Leek and Westbourne hit-men come to collect on the molars alone. "Perhaps there's some mistake."

"Look," I said. "I've had a tough day. I just now impounded a stereo outfit almost the size of Hilversum. I twisted my wrist putting some hi-fi jerk into Casualty, not to mention the weight of his appliance could really louse up the dampers on what is a personal, paid-up, fully-owned sedan of mine right across the street. On top of which, I have to have some defaulter's entire apartment distrained and it seems nobody has thought to tell him I bruise easily. Lady, you don't know the half of it, so don't push me."

"I don't know about that," she said. "But I shouldn't leave your car over there if I was you. There's charging on even dates. Will you excuse me, please, only I've something on the stove."

The showdown

I SIGHED. Nothing changes in the debt-collecting business. I let go with my pack of guarantee cards and the breeze caught her aerodynamics; she backed off. At least my feet were spared this time out. I took hold of a shoulder-strap and put her and the dress back on the rail. Useful feature in these older properties: they were built with the kind of picture-rail can take the strain. She made some cute little dangle-dolly. "Pardon me," I breathed, "before lunch I wear my chivalry thin."

I figured the laundry would be out back. It'd help a lot to have a dog I could train to maybe sniff out the Persil Automatic, give me some edge on the situation. As it turned out, the undersigned was out back all right but in a single room was doubling as a kitchenette and TV lounge. To start with it looked as if he was going to play easy and cool. "Meter's in the cupboard," was all he said.

"The fridge," I said, keeping my shoulders loose. "You're behind on the instalments. It goes unless there's cash on the nail. From tomorrow, buster, the Laundromat, programme ten."

He stood up. There are, I suppose, many reasons why a person should stand up. Only one of these reasons, I acknowledge, is maybe to argue with a man who's sent to collect. One reason is enough, we don't take chances any longer. I dived in low, took him by the knees and zapped him across the table and on to the drier's Melamine top before he had time to try on anything smart. The model IV is castorised, I knew. We cruised clean through the scullery door and into the alleyway, the undersigned I dropped off on the compost pile and had the appliance steered round the front and into the sedan before he had time to call up any support.

Just another job. I wasn't looking forward to the next one, though. Dish-washers more than ten days over are always tough.

STANLEY by Murray Ball

Featuring the adventures of the Great Palaeolithic Hero

135

"It's your round."

"It's an inflationary little wine, I'm afraid, sir."

"Mine too—every week it's 'meat's gone up'—'clothing's gone up'—'rent's going up' . . . ."

"I'm afraid, sir, that you must blame VAT for these new price rises—that will be ten pence, please."

"I made my pile before inflation—now I'm having to remake it every year!"

"Eight quid. Say ten quid. Make it easier to work out the VAT on it."

"Today we'll tackle percentages."

"I hate to do this, but I've just taken on a huge mortgage."

"Not to worry—with every mortgage we give free hormone injections to ensure longevity."

"In what outrageous price bracket, sir?"

"What you lose in exchange rates is more than made up by missing two week's price rises!"

"We must apologise for the delay in your flight and that during the delay the cost of your trip has gone up by 20 per cent."

"And if you thought those prices in Germany and Holland were high, just look at these in Paris!"

Bring me my bars of burning gold, Bring me my ingots of desire...

Great poems of the Money Crisis

Darling, I am growing old, let us join the flight to gold!
Death is grinning at the gate—look at this conversion rate!
But, my darling, if we flee to a gold-based currency,
O how happy we shall be! We may yet survive Phase Three.

●

(In affectionate memory of a great monetary conference)
O Bretton Woods were heaven!
And jocund were the nights.
In nineteen-forty-seven
We talked the world to rights.
The structure we erected
Is gone and hardly missed,
And here we stand rejected,
Our knickers in a twist.
In Bretton Woods, half-witted,
We quaffed the flowing cup.
Too bad that we omitted
To string each other up.

●

The Pound is going it alone,
Doodah, doodah!
The Pound is sinking like a stone,
Doodah, doodah, day!
Goin' to sink some more,
Goin' to fade away!
The Pound has fallen through the floor,
Doodah, doodah, day!

●

I'm a silly little kroner.
I'm an outcast, I'm a loner.
No one wants to purchase me,
I'm as useless as can be.
Toora loora loora lee!

(Pivot on last line, with forefinger on head)
          Repeat with:
          I'm a potty little quetzal,
          Frankly, I'm not worth a pretzel.
          I'm a dreary old escudo,
          Only fit for playing Ludo.
          I'm a randy little rand,
          Who will take me by the hand?
          I'm a drachma—yoo hoo hoo!
          Do I stink? I'll say I do, etc. etc.

                    ●

O say, can you see by the dawn's early light
    The vision we hailed as disaster seemed nearing?
The Dollar advancing with God-given might,
    Enfeebled no more by the Watergate hearing?
O say, do the dime and the quarter still flash
In the land of the tough and the home of the brash?
Does Europe still bow, as it did long ago,
At the sight of a greenback? Well, actually, no.

                    ●

Just a dream of comfort, when the larder's low,
While the Central Bankers vainly come and go.
Just a sigh for prices soaring past recall,
Just a dream of ease, dear, just a dream, that's all.

                    ●

Come all ye bold rascals and list to my lay.
I move my hot money by night and by day.
From pesos to guilders, from guilders to Marks—
This short-term investment's the choicest of larks!
I'm two jumps ahead of the Council of Ten,
I laugh as they try realigning the yen.
The "snake in the tunnel" means nothing to me.
Let crawling pegs crawl—I am footloose and free.
So come, ye bold rascals, and heed not the rage
Of all the dull boneheads who work for a wage.
And lose not your nerve when the storm flags are blowing:
When the going gets tough, it's the tough who get going!

                    ●

          Children of a future age
          Reading this immortal page
          Know that in a former time
          Thrift was punished for a crime.
          Those who saved with might and main
          Lost their money down the drain.
          This was due to Market Forces.
          Children, why not back the horses?

                              E. S. TURNER

President Ford has asked the American Society of Composers and Performers to get the lads to write a few anti-inflation numbers. What have our own bards been doing? E. S. TURNER starts the ball rolling.

COME all ye bold blockheads and hark to my lay!
Our foe is Inflation, the fiend we must slay.
Call off all your pickets, withdraw all your claims,
And spend less on petrol, and bitter, and dames.

You say that Inflation's a beautiful sight!
It wipes out the savings of all who vote Right.
It clobbers the thrifty, a grand thing to do,
But oh, you thick oafs, it will bury you too!

You tell us Inflation's the road to content,
With wages all rising one hundred per cent,
And Doctor and Parson ground down in the dust,
But we'll all be alike when the country goes bust.

And what will you do then, you obstinate dolts?
You'll stage a last sit-in and eat nuts and bolts.
A pensionless nation will wallow in blood.
I tell you, Inflation will do you no good!

So come to my standard, all girt for the fray,
We'll fight this Inflation the whole of the way.
Just string up your leaders, or coat them in tar,
And the world will then see what grand fellows you are!

HARK, I hear the trumpets sounding,
  Shrilly, in the battle's dawn!
All Inflation's guns are pounding,
  All the swords of Greed are drawn.
In my ears the blood is singing;
  Mother, I am feeling faint.
But I rise and give a ringing
  Call for Voluntary Restraint.

Mockingly the foe advances,
  Jeering at my heartfelt call.
Blood is on the union lances,
  Bourgeois blood, the best of all.
Mother, now behold me lying
  Sacrificed, without complaint!
From my lips there comes a dying
  Call for Voluntary Restraint.

I am numbered with the martyrs,
  On my name there is no strain.
They have got my guts for garters,
  But I did not die in vain.
I have left a star to steer by.
  Some day I shall be a saint.
Some day, somebody will hear my
  Call for Voluntary Restraint.

NOW winter strips the hedges,
  The buds of hope are dead,
And some men jump from ledges,
  And some from Beachy Head.

In snivelling battalions
  The brokers are in flight,
With sacks of gold medallions
  Against the Fall of Night.

No herds are left for farming,
  And blasted is the heath.
The self-employed are arming,
  With daggers in their teeth.

O proud and dismal Nation,
  O Nation without friend,
How then shall dread Inflation
  Be conquered at the end?

Have done with vile excesses!
  Put greed and graft to rout!
Blow up your printing presses
  That roll the banknotes out!

Dismiss your maddened spenders,
  Cut down the trash you eat,
Say no to Arab lenders,
  And stand on your own feet!

PUT your arms around me, honey,
  Soothe me with your gentle hands.
Let us try to spend our money
  Only upon Krugerrands.

Lean your head against me, baby,
  Do not vex me with demands.
If we pinch and scrape, then maybe
  We can buy more Krugerrands.

Kiss my throbbing temples, cutie,
  Surely cutie understands
It's a prudent lover's duty
  To invest in Krugerrands.

When we face the death of money,
  Wasted cities, worthless lands,
Shall we not be thankful, honey,
  That we bought up Krugerrands.

"We've decided to absorb increased costs ourselves, Jackson, rather than pass them on to the customer— you're fired!"

"The moderates, I feel, would be prepared to keep their unreasonable demands within limits."

"There must be some misunderstanding—the three and a half
million was just for the model."

"We're moving into commodities, Fribton—convert
all those blocks of luxury flats back into old warehouses."

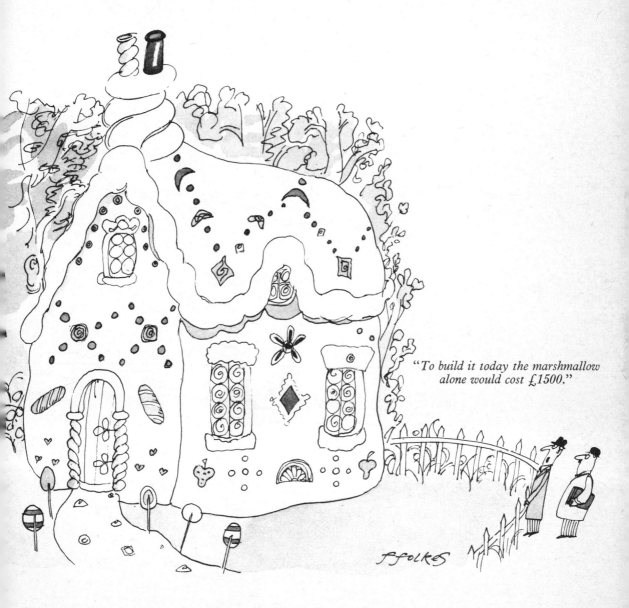

"*To build it today the marshmallow alone would cost £1500.*"

ffolkes

SHOCK RISE IN PETROL PRICES-

AND THERE'S MORE TO COME!

throughout the country today the picture was the same. Panic, gloom, despair, abandoned cars and chronic hyperbole gripped the nation as prices on all grades of petrol took a further giddy spiralling upward leap-frog. Distraught forecourt attendants walked away from their pumps and, picking a route through the stranded hardware, expressed fears of a return to the sudden widespread up-surge in "gazumping"—motorists who promise substantial amounts in cash and collateral to order a fill-up and then drive off at the last moment when they are offered more attractive terms at alter-native pumps. "It's the same old story of supply and demand, maybe it's destiny, who knows?" commented one stunned garage proprietor.

Already in the southern counties and in many major cities, an RAC spokesman has described the situation as "chaotic" with some garages on the A5 offering a free Mini with every six gallons of 5-star. Said one garage on the A5 today: "It's desperate." The AA called it diabolical and warned: "It's going to get worse!" as two and three mile queues built up in the rush-hour at banks and second-mortgage houses where worried motorists fought a last-minute battle at the eleventh hour to secure loans with which to "top up" before tomorrow's grim round of announcements of further swinging in-creases is made.

Motorists wept to hear of one bright chink of encouragement which appeared through the encircling black despair. Pensioner Lawrence "Jim" Hersch, 88, of The Black Cat Barbershop, Batley-on-Ouse, won £355,000 44p on the Treble Chance and declared to excited crowds in Batley-on-Ouse's prestigious Clare-mont Rooms: "It's like a dream come true. Straightaway my son has taught me the controls, I plan to blow the lot on a motoring tour of the Yorkshire Dales."

53

PETROL PRICE SHOCK!

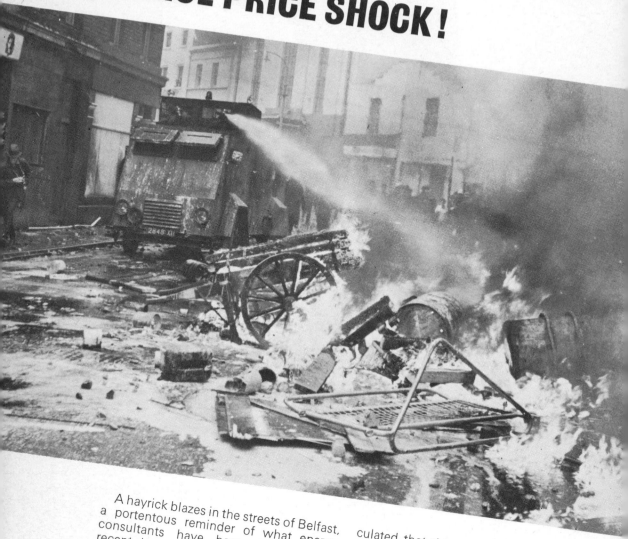

A hayrick blazes in the streets of Belfast, a portentous reminder of what energy consultants have been predicting in recent days. As all but the richest nations begin puttering to a halt, it has been widely acknowledged that prohibitive costs may bring about a sudden and dramatic decline in the number of incidents of urban terrorism in Northern Ireland and elsewhere involving the hurling of petrol bombs or the movement of booby-trapped cars. It has been calculated that the way things are going it will soon become economically more viable for guerillas to supply and equip an entire infantry regiment or small sailing fleet than foot the bill for a whole milk bottle of petroleum, even 2-star. And while motor-cars are expected to remain readily available for loose change, their movement to a suitable location for combustion is fast becoming beyond the means of all but the super powers.

"The sky is falling! The sky is falling!"

A NATION OF GREENFINGERS

With food prices escalating daily, the Government's Phase Four will now consist of a compulsory grow-it-yourself policy. MAHOOD reports from the top of the compost heap.

"I've turned the front and back lawns over to wheat and if there's a glut the Russians will always take it off my hands."

"Now he lives in constant fear of a plague of locusts!"

NO COVETING

"I'm sorry, I can't help you—I've had to plough in my cannabis crop and plant bloody spuds!"

"I don't mind the extra work, it's the cluck cluck here, the cluck cluck there, here a cluck, there a cluck, everywhere a cluck cluck, that's driving me mad!"

"For God's sake, Robert, the curfew tolled the knell of parting day hours ago!"

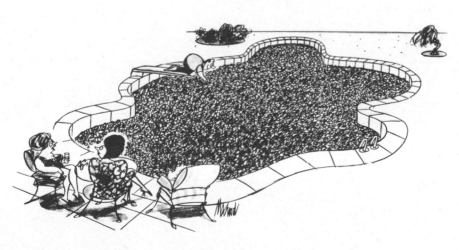

"What Henry doesn't understand is that when it comes to water-cress one **doesn't** think big!"

Tighten your belts please BY GRAHAM

"And you, Margaret? . . . Rhubarb or elderberry?"

"We can't eat roses, Felicity."

"I think it's quite good, considering I've never made a suit before."

"Good God! The Joneses are filling in their swimming pool."

"I **am** the Marchioness!"

"Hello Mother, it's me . . . How are you? Good . . . we're all fine . . . Goodbye."

"Press on, lads, press on."

"It's a common complaint these days—
try and stay away from rampant
inflation for a month or two."

CROSS YOUR CHEQUE AND HOPE TO DIE

SHERIDAN MORLEY on the funeral business

IT'S not the cost of living I worry about, nor even the cost of dying—it's the cost of being dead. Morbid curiosity, I suppose, but ever since Jessica Mitford surveyed the American way of death I've been worrying about my own. What price a grave nowadays, and what guarantee that once I'm in it they won't move me to make way for a motorway?

In time of such mental anguish, I usually ring Harrods. It is possible, you know, to live and die by Harrods. They won't actually bring you into the world but once you are in it they'll provide (indeed I once had a cousin who verified this) everything you could conceivably need up to and beyond the grave. On this occasion, however, they were less than forthcoming: "*We prefer not to discuss burial costs unless of course it's an immediate grave you'll be requiring—they do tend to vary in price and in any case the longer you leave it the more expensive it's going to be.*"

Unreassured, I pressed on to the National Association of Funeral Directors but they were out for lunch and for that matter tea and breakfast as well . . . either that or I'd hit an unprecedentedly busy time for carting the stiffs.

Highgate Cemetery wasn't much more helpful: they're closed to new customers, though they've still got some room reserved for those far-sighted enough to book in advance. Price? They weren't saying, but they did refer me to St. Pancras which is where they also seem to refer those who leave their bookings until the last minute, so to speak. St. Pancras say they can reserve you a nice site for around £35, though it'll cost at least another £30 or so to get into it.

But once I'm there, what happens? I don't mean what happens to me personally, since I'd rather not think about that, but what happens if my heirs decide I'm taking up a useful building site or that they'd get a good price for the land elsewhere? Can one buy and sell grave plots, or is necro-speculation not yet one of the acceptable faces of capitalism?

"Now that's what I call value for money."

Those funeral directors to whom I talked (and they were a singularly uncommunicative lot, the result presumably of years spent staring mournfully into gaping holes in the ground) took the view that once you'd got a grave you'd got a grave, and that there wasn't much either the church or your family could do about it except maybe shove a few more relatives in on top. Nevertheless one or two did admit that grave sites had been known to change hands privately although they saw no immediate likelihood of whole graveyards being turned over to the builders of desirable town houses. Still, as one said wistfully, "Has anyone ever thought what Highgate Cemetery would fetch on the open market?"

Mind you, the relatives wouldn't care for it—at least not all of them. In America five years ago when they (disastrously) turned Evelyn Waugh's *The Loved One* into a film the script-writer Terry Southern came up with the idea that in order to make better use of graveyards for property development all corpses should in future be sealed in capsules and sent into permanent orbit around the earth. When the movie was released, American undertakers received dozens of complaints—and hundreds of enquiries about how soon it could be done.

Other countries, other customs: nevertheless a Cornish undertaker is reputed to have announced recently that his clients could only be sure of retaining their graves "for life" though he did refrain from announcing, in the words of one celebrated Californian cemetery, that all graves had a clear sea view.

Evidently this country is still hopelessly behind in Deathbiz; why, for instance, is there no English edition of *Concept: The Journal of Creative Ideas For Cemeteries* which, published in Los Angeles, notes that it is possible to get 1800 graves (only they prefer to call them "plantings") into an acre and to charge upwards of five hundred dollars for each one? What with that and *Mortuary Management* (which still refers to the author of *The Loved One* as "Evelyn-bites-the-hands-that-feed-him-Waugh") American undertakers are infinitely better off than our own men in black. They have no less than nine other trade papers advising them on how to pre-sell graves, together with notes on how to avoid ugly scenes with vicars, florists, cremation enthusiasts, etc.

A place like Forest Lawn for instance, the apotheosis of the grave industry, doesn't hold with scattering ashes:

"Recognizable fragments of the human frame," says their brochure, "that come hurtling out of the skies, wash ashore on beaches or roll about underfoot in gardens and parks appal the strangers who encounter them and cause lifelong heartache to those who have had any share in such disposition of a loved one's remains."

Besides, cremations are bad for business. On the other hand, what if they run out of grave sites before I'm ready for mine? Living as I do quite close to our village church, I made a few discreet enquiries of the Vicar. I am not a small person, and the churchyard is already looking pretty crowded considering the first lot got in there around 1420 and started putting up vast great concrete slabs over their heads so we'd know who they were.

He, the Vicar that is, seemed to think he might have room for me round behind the pub, where there's a kind of graveyard annexe; that seems to be about the most I can hope for.

Somehow though I can't help envying the Californians; not for them the indignities of touting yourself around neighbouring graveyards, measuring yourself as I do by lying flat on apparently available bits of turf and seeing if your toes stick out over anyone else's post-humous property. There, it's all done by memorial counsellors who appear to have been trained in the arts of showmanship by the late Florenz Ziegfield himself. The trouble is of course that we die too quietly over here: I fully hope and intend that when I go it will be noisily. All the same, it's a grave outlook.

TOO PROUD
TO BEG
Please
help me
buy a
gun

Hallowood

"The British now say that they can't afford our report on their economic future."

"Live within our means! My God, don't say it's come to that."

"*Don't spend too much time reading it. The first payment is nearly due.*"

"*I know exactly what you're all thinking. You're thinking 'He's going to talk yet again about the dreadfully boring business of inflation.' Well, I've got a surprise for you. I'm not going to talk about inflation: I'm going to talk about reflation.*"

"*I can't help wondering just how much all the worldly goods I renounced might be worth now.*"

"Very interesting I'm sure, sir. Now if I could just expound the monetarist argument . . ."

"You'll just have to work faster to keep pace with inflation."

PART 3
STOP THE SPIRAL
—I WANT TO
GET OFF

"Do you haggle?"

HOW CAN I BEAT INFLATION –

without buying a lot of awful pictures called 'Now comes still evening on' and 'The sun is in his western bower'? Eh?

I want to be one of those hard-faced men who prosper in times of inflation and finish up with peacocks on the lawn. What should I do?

You should start writing articles called "How YOU Can Beat Inflation." Fleet Street pays up to £40 a time for them and it's a real growth industry. Also it's easier than digging coal.

You don't mean all those articles telling people to collect antiques and postage stamps and Roman ear-picks and old manhole covers? I wouldn't know how to begin.

You begin: "In times when money loses twenty per cent of its value every year the shrewd investor puts his faith in time-honoured valuables which maintain their worth even in the worst financial blizzards."

I don't think I could bring myself to say that. Is it really any use collecting old manhole covers?

Of course not. But it gives people confidence, takes their mind off inflation and prevents widespread unrest.

Except among those whose bread-winners fall down manholes.

Please. Let us try to keep this on a responsible level. You mentioned peacocks earlier.

That's right. I had just read about a man who drove a flock of three thousand peacocks through Trebizond—

A splendid sight, I'm sure. You are quite right to say that there are always hard-faced men with peacocks on their lawns—

Then I should collect peacocks?

No, but you should write an article "Invest In Peacocks Now" or "Keep Wolves At Bay The Peacock Way". Editors are desperate for stuff like that.

68

You don't think I should go out and really collect something?

Not unless you can think of something so utterly useless, something so profoundly undesirable that nobody else would ever hit on it. That's how fortunes are made.

What about fruiterers' labels, the ones which say "Please Don't Squeeze Me Until I'm Yours" or "Choice Navels"?

Too late. Everybody's collecting stuff like that.

Then what about glossy photographs of unit trust chairmen? Or signed glossy photographs of Peter Walker?

You're getting the idea. That could be the great camp craze of tomorrow. But I'll give you one piece of advice.

Yes?

Don't bother buying up paintings of Liverpool Zoo animals by the Victorian artist William Huggins, because Mrs. Jackie Onassis is already cornering them. It says so here in the Sunday Times.

You mean Mrs. Onassis, with all her wealth, is having to put her faith in pictures of crocodiles in Liverpool Zoo? Things must be far worse than I thought.

It also says Jim Slater is buying up Victorian landscapes by some goof called Watts. As you know, Slater is chairman of the Slater-Walker empire, but he's looking for something which will hold its value.

I'm really getting the wind up. What puzzles me is this: when the real German-style inflation comes, how do you turn pictures of crocodiles into bread and butter? Suppose I've got this Important Collection of Old English Mangles coming up at Sotheby's, but I'm hungry, really hungry. Money's no use to me.

To save you from financial ruin: Four famous experts in the field of art, antiques and confidence trickery offer advice on what to collect in these difficult times.

For me (writes Sebastian Quint) the future lies in old pulpits and/or confessional boxes (preferably with the red lights still working). They can be picked up quite easily in the "flea markets" of Italy by anyone who has the foresight to go on holiday with a pantechnicon or two. When money finally collapses I expect the world to beat a pathway to my door.

Not everyone looking for a hedge against inflation automatically thinks of Bellamy's Patented African Carrier, a useful bygone from Empire-building days and still used in Rhodesia to this day (writes Rupert Gall). The Carrier cost £5 15s new and today is literally priceless. No one need ever starve with a hangar full of Bellamy's Carriers. Unloaded discreetly on the market in times of crisis, they are the perfect weapon against inflation, famine and pestilence.

Please. Let us not cross our bridges before we come to them.

I thought you would say that. Have you any other ideas for surviving inflation, apart from collecting old rubbish?

Yes. Have you ever thought of creating rubbish? I mean handicrafts. Hand-made goods always keep their value. It doesn't matter how crude they are. Lopsided bowls, scratchy plates with clumsy designs, horrible, lumpy, hand-woven tweed—the craft shops are full of stuff like that. People will always prefer the hand-botched job to the smooth, efficient, factory article.

But I can't stick two bits of wood together without them falling apart.

You sound just the stuff of which craftsmen are made. Keep at it.

Might there not be a craze some day for well-designed, factory-made cups and saucers?

I wouldn't count on it. Collectors aren't fools, you know.

You're sure?

70

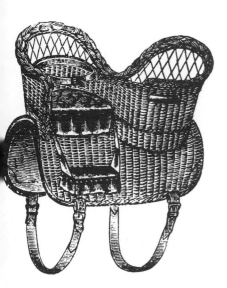

Victorian double-chair facing-both-ways saddles for children are much sought after (writes Vince Rope) and I count myself fortunate in possessing the only one in existence. Do not listen to those who would fob you off with a Bellamy's Patented African Carrier, a useless piece of Africana if ever I saw one.

What is more aesthetically and functionally satisfying than a good spiral staircase? If you choose your specimens carefully (writes Bert Rumble) they will fit into each other, thus simplifying storage problems. When you have collected a "nest" of about fifty the quality Sunday papers will write them up and your investment will quadruple overnight.

Of course, one classic way to offset inflation is to keep your wife working at full stretch. Her main job should be in a good food store, where she will be allowed to buy stale pies cheap at the end of the day.

I didn't bring ten children into the world to eat stale pies.

If you have ten children, you're home and dry. Send them all to work, as soon as possible, for different airlines, then you can travel at negligible family rates all over the world, eating free meals and consuming duty-free liquor. Already hundreds are finding it's cheaper than staying at home.

I thought you would have mentioned gold by now.

There are tiresome restrictions on gold. But there's nothing to stop you filling your mouth with gold teeth before each flight and having them pulled out and banked in Zurich.

Well, thanks. I think I'd rather collect old bicycle pumps. On second thoughts, I'll collect articles on how to beat inflation.

MOVE ALONG THERE, CONSTABLE!

DAVID TAYLOR finds that beauty is in the eye of the investor

BEWILDERING, capricious, snob-ridden, daft; deadlocks mitred into every toughened door, bells that set up clanging in the middle of the night; insurers wake up sweating that a fag might brush the wall, it's like owning a priceless, fussy pet that is wonderful to look at but it can't abide the damp; art as an investment is not something you could happily recommend to anyone less than stinking rich and lucky, or touched with second sight, or just touched. The market has long since tumbled anyway that more or less anything goes, and generally goes for a pretty fancy price, so that it could happen any day that the buyers will tumble too.

Meantime, it's boom time with works of art showing all the signs of turning to sophisticated currency: sales worth £18 million notched up in a single season at Sotheby's alone, bold canvases splodged evenly with a monochrome hue are up to 600 dollars for every square foot; £33,000 for a porcelain horse.

In the established world of genius, the stakes and the compound risks are getting heftier every day. People are queuing up to buy clockworks, miniatures, itsy-bitsy *objets d'art*, anything, in fact, that is readily stashed. And it's anybody's guess how the possible returns might jump. The word is certainly out that there are profits to be made if you can only hang on to the stuff, and it doesn't take an aesthete to spot that leaping prices have ceased to have much truck with recognised standards of judgement or of taste. There is a definite sniff about of trends and capital gains. And the purists are appalled.

"Great pictures, we are told, are for buying and selling, for putting into portfolios (of a kind) and for providing dividends," ran a recent snorting letter to *The Times*, "The money-changers are established in the temple. The shame of it, O Rembrandt, the pity of it, Fra Angelico!" Sir Charles Wheeler, PPRA, was thus amongst the vanguard of chi-chi distaste for this sudden surge of something less than arty fascination that has lately gripped such a sensitive zone.

72

It is still plenty sensitive enough for Sotheby's to declare that anyone involved in the art world doesn't really countenance the field of art as investment.

You're doing this for pleasure, understand. Sotheby's dealer David Ellis-Jones can keep a perfectly straight face and announce: "If anyone walks in and says, look, I've got £50,000 and I want to invest it in art, I would say that's not our job." Speculation nothing, you have got to like the thing. The risks are your own affair. The gentlemen in the trade require that you should know what it is you like and when your taste is declared they will advise you what it's worth. Full-stop and good morning.

It is astonishing the numbers of sober, level businessmen who have come to discover that their tastes are more refined than ever they had supposed, now that the market is ablaze. As in any roaring blaze, fingers do get burnt but vulgar charts and analyses have lately begun to take up space in the heavier papers to advise against the risks. Nevertheless, the widespread assumption persists that it is a long way short of decent to suppose that art has any connection at all with a thing quite so common as cash, dear me, no.

Doubtless the recent shiftings about of capital have their own peculiar logic but it must always be acknowledged that matters concerning works of art and their so-rewarding aesthetics simply blossom like the daffodils. People purchase paintings only to assuage their culture-lust, they buy only what they like. Ask anybody working in the trade.

I put this point to property-tycoon Ronnie Lyon who maintains a collection and a very soft spot for Lowry. He admitted that it sometimes worried him sick, but, "I suppose that

"All that stuff pays the rent, of course, but I keep the important things over here."

it's a hobby. When one is buying expensive pictures, I think that one has to pay some regard to the values out of sheer common sense," he said, "but I certainly wouldn't make that the dominant factor, I never think of investment. At all."

Gerald Reitlinger is a man who seems to think of little else, and has produced three sturdy volumes on the jumpiness of economics and taste. Alongside carefully tabulated lists of what fetched what and where, he concludes that people have been buying paintings for fabulous sums since the middle of the last century, and that given the complicated shiftings of what money is worth, what it could buy, and how much of it is, and was, in a position to be easily got, values haven't changed that much. Not in money, anyway.

He also notes that if the figures are to be believed, the following, in strict order of rotation, are the greatest English painters of the past 100 years: Sargent, Sir Alfred Munnings, Francis Bacon, Sir Winston Churchill. Try to pick the winners if you can. Briefly, Reitlinger stresses that the recent, sudden inflation has wrought havoc on the sales and he gets particularly shirty over the deliberate and indoctrinated confusion of artistic appreciation with self-interest, a tendency that leads in the end to the corrosion of civilised living, to the everlasting bonfire of speculative gain. The very thought sends him wild.

I asked another collector-businessman, Sir Charles Forte, if the tendency worried him. Not a bit. "Why shouldn't people buy paintings instead of pieces of silver, or bars of gold?" he said. "My own particular view, of course, is that the value of artistic things is entirely in the pleasure you derive from them." Of course. Sir Charles is another Lowry fan. Reitlinger dismisses Lowry by remarking that, "An easily perceived quaintness, a not too strident proletarian emphasis and absolutely no surprises whatever, these are the right qualities for a provincial public—and enough to lift this painter in the course of a decade from the £300 region to the £8,000 region."

"If you concentrate very hard it turns into a cheque for £50,000."

But for Sir Charles Forte, there is a certain satisfaction in the way that this man paints, and he doesn't mind much that the price is going up either. "I think I would be over-modest if I said that I wasn't pleased at having had the good taste to buy a man who has been proved good by the market." And he's still on the up. Ronnie Lyon confirms that in Lowry, "There is a man of many moods. Basically, I think he is trying to portray the romance of the dull little man, who is a man for all that. When you really look at them, there is an awful lot there." Enough, certainly, for Mr. Lyon's latest acquisition to have boosted the price of Lowry to the £16,000 region.

"One tries," says Arthur Davidson from the gallery of that name, "not to be greedy. Most of our customers these days are wealthy and shrewd businessmen. They have a pretty good idea what a thing is worth, perhaps they can't judge it to a fiver, but pretty good. They will say if a thing's too dear." Not so in the auction rooms. David Ellis-Jones at Sotheby's estimates on whether he can get the given price or not. Up at the top, he alleged, "There isn't much difference between £50,000 or £70,000."

It doesn't really do for us to linger on that point, but he told me a story to show the wisdom of his schemes. "I know two pop singers," he said, "who I wouldn't have thought had the first clue about art. There are in the entertainment industry, they probably come from, God knows, North country backgrounds; they had a pretty miserable childhood, and let's say they made their money in clubs and that sort of thing. They have bought at Sotheby's, on instinct, *fabulous* things. They picked out the best things in the sale, just incredible. Marvellous. One loved it."

You pays your money and you takes your choice—picking only what you like, of course. It is, says Sotheby's, *terribly* difficult to know what's good, even though some pop singers apparently have the knack. Ronnie Lyon feels the difficulty, too, and revealed that he was

"Gold leaf! More gold leaf!"

only recently prepared to go as much as £50,000 or £70,000 (for the difference, see above) over and above what he thought a certain painting was worth, but he wouldn't stretch to what he considered was a price £200,000 over the odds, the price which the picture finally fetched. "I think it is emotion," he said.

Confusion, then, undoubtedly is rife, to the extent that *The Times* sale-room correspondent was recently shaken enough to divulge that, "It is a feature of auctions that some surprisingly low prices are combined with some surprisingly high." How true that is. So why does anyone bother?

Pride of ownership, perhaps. That is beginning to wear thin now that the thieves have shown up the old theory that first-class paintings have no commodity value to be as dead as the sensible price-tag. "What do they *do* with them?" Ronnie Lyon asked, aghast. No doubt, someone, somewhere *has* made enormous profits by keeping an eye to fashionable trends, but Reitlinger warns that, "Individual pretentiousness in the arts has progressed far beyond what were once reckoned to be the frontiers of sanity." Bewildering, capricious, snob-ridden, daft; insurers and Securicor rushed off their feet. No-one that I talked to ever thought about the prospects of selling off their wares. David Ellis-Jones came closest when he said that some of his customers might now and then vouchsafe that their tastes had suddenly changed. He wouldn't accept, when pressed, though, that it came to a nice kind of euphemism for saying that the market was going stale. Arthur Davidson added cryptically that there was a tendency in some businesses to feel that they were simply not in trade.

"The market," Sotheby's says, "looks after itself, you see. Let's hope that people learn something from coming to Sotheby's."

Let's hope so. Better go and check, meanwhile, that the latch is on the door. Interest in the finer things is growing every day.

*"Number twenty-nine. Simply
entitled 'Hedge Against Inflation'!"*

SO WE'LL ALL PULL TOGETHER

The Headmaster of Eton has suggested that one of the ways for the public schools to fight the effects of inflation would be for the pupils to do the maintenance work themselves. Does he realise, asks ALAN COREN, what that could lead to?

QUELCH was waxy! He paced the rug of his study, beetle-browed! He swished about with his cane!

He stopped. His oaken door had suddenly swung open! There had been no knock, but Quelch could not bother with such trifles now!

"Cherry!" exclaimed Quelch.

"Morning, squire," said Bob Cherry. He came into the room, and dropped his toolbag on the rug.

"Look here, Cherry," stormed the beak, "I made it absolutely clear that I required IMMEDIATE repairs to my gas fire! Three days have passed, and this is the first I've seen of you. Do you have any explanation?"

Bob Cherry took off his cap, blew his nose into it thoughtfully, and put it back on again.

"You don't want to look a gift horse in the wossname, son," he said. "You're dead lucky I come at all. We're up to here with bleeding orders, aren't we? Time of year. First cold snap, every Tom, Dick and Auntie Freda's on the blower, know what I mean? I trust you're keeping the brass monkey well wrapped up, squire, ha-ha-ha, nudge, nudge, get it? Brass monkey, wrapped up, catch my drift?"

Quelch fumed! The famous Quelch cheeks went purple! But what could the baleful beak *do*?

"Pah! Just get on with it, Cherry!"

Whereupon Quelch hurled himself into his chair, peering in silent fury over his spectacles as the irrepressible Bob munched his cheese sandwiches, filled in his pools coupon, perused his *Sun*, and finally ripped up the carpet in front of the fire.

"Yes, werl, it's prob'ly your brass union," said Cherry, "I'll have to lift your boards."

Whereupon he tore up four or five of the hallowed Greyfriars timbers, and began jabbing into the cavity beneath with his cold chisel.

"Oy!" cried Cherry.

He leapt back! From the gaping hole in Quelch's floor, a fountain of water spurted up like a jolly old geyser. Which certainly isn't the way the casual spectator would have described Mr. Quelch! He reeled! He boggled!

"*What—is—that*?" he spluttered.

"That's only your bleeding water main, innit?" shouted Cherry. "Diabolical, running under the floor like that, right next to your gas conduit!"

At which he gathered his tools together, chucked them into his bag, and made for the door!

"Where on earth do you think you're going?" cried Quelch, as the grubby water rose swirling about his august ankles.

Bob Cherry turned.

"If you think I'm going to work in conditions like this," he said, "you got another think coming, mate!"

"Excuse me, please," said Hurree Jamset Ram Singh, "but I was just asking myself whether perhaps you would be requiring some small assistance with . . ."

Johnny Bull slid his head out from beneath the Headmaster's Cortina.

"Only bleeding word you lot know," he said, "assistance! Get off the curry boat and it's Excuse me, but where is the Assistance is what I am asking, where is the incredible free handing out, where . . ."

"Coming over here," said Lord Mauleverer, who was drowsing in the back seat, a plug-spanner in his lap, "taking our jobs from under our noses, sleeping with our fags, dragging the country down. Go on, sod off!"

"It is not like that at all," protested the dusky chap, "it is not like that in any way whatsoever! My father happens to be a maharajah, and . . ."

"Then clear orf out of it!" cried Harry Wharton, who was crouching over the beak's fuel tank, a length of rubber hose dangling from his mouth. "We don't want to catch nuffink!"

"I was merely wishing to inform you that Dr. Locke respectfully asks when his motor car will be ready," murmured the Indian fellow, "He is pointing out where you have had it for two weeks now."

"We're waiting for spares, aren't we?" exclaimed Johnny Bull. "There's a bottleneck up the factory, right? It's the three-day week, innit, plus snow on the points at Didcot, not to mention the Eyetalian dock strike. Okay?"

"But you are only supposed to be cleaning it," pointed out the persistent Inky.

Johnny Bull eased himself out completely, and removed the trannie button from his ear.

"They're bleeding amazing, these people, aren't they?" he cried.

Harry Wharton shook his tousled head! He grinned his famous grin! He put his sturdy arm around the Indian chap's shoulder!

"Look, my old wog son, we need *wheels*, don't we? We have to get *about*, right? Finish Simonizing old Lockie's banger, where are we, know what I mean?"

Hurree Jamset Ram Singh shrugged, and ambled away! The three chums watched him become a sidling speck! Lord Mauleverer sighed his famous sigh!

"Ready for integration?" he snorted. "I should cocoa! I wouldn't send 'em up to get coconuts!"

The Remove filed into their maths class. The Remove sat down. The Remove looked at the blackboard.

The Remove gasped!

Harry Wharton stood up.

"Who done that board?" he enquired.

"I beg your pardon?" said Mr. Tremlowe.

"The board," said Wharton. "It's been wiped. What my hon. executive and me wish to know is who done it? Last night, there wasn't a clean spot on it, right, brothers?"

"Right!" cried the Remove.

"If you must know," said Mr. Tremlowe, "I cleaned it myself."

You could have heard the proverbial pin drop!

"Right," said Harry Wharton, at last, "you heard him, brothers!"

Whereupon the Remove stood up again, and began to walk out!

"Where are you going?" cried Mr. Tremlowe.

Wharton paused at the master's dais. Beneath his safety helmet, his honest young face had gone scarlet!

"That board," he muttered, "that *board*, is only to be cleaned by a duly accredited and assigned Chalk Removal Operative, to wit, Lord Mauleverer, as per our directive of the fourteenth ultimo, *what has been circulated to all managerial staff!*"

"Taking bread out of the proletariat's mouth!" exclaimed Lord Mauleverer. "Harking back to the worst bleeding excesses of Tsarist Belgium!"

"Russia!" hissed Harry Wharton.

"*And* them!" said Mauly.

"They'll be opening their own bloody windows next," cried the Hon. Jack Armstrong.

The Remove marched out, as one man.

But what, I hear the reader pondering, what of Bunter? What of the Famous Owl, what of that fatuous fattie, that ridiculous rotundity, that benighted blot on the Greyfriars landscape?

Bunter was in bed! Bunter snored! Bunter burbled in his slumber, dreaming as only Bunter could dream, of even less work, even more scoff, even more scrounging, even more money arriving in envelopes from even more gullible sources!

And nobody, of course, dared to disturb him, or criticise him, or kick the fat Bunter behind.

He was, after all, the School hero.

Art today,
dividends tomorrow

MAHOOD reports

"We are expecting a dramatic rise
in his prices at any moment."

"Actually, I'm one of your patrons—my
unit trust owns a piece of you."

"That Picasso-Annigoni
merger—it never really
worked."

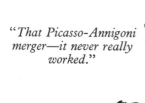

"*I don't understand it, but it's doing a damn sight better than my Marks and Sparks.*"

"*When Jim Slater starts to paint—that's when I'll start to buy.*"

"*Whose bright idea was it to use cheap fugitive colours? We've had to recall five hundred damn landscapes for Sutherland to repaint!*"

High-flying speculators are making fortunes on the commodity market in America, notably by buying soya beans they never see and don't want. How is it done? A financial wizard who wishes to remain anonymous offers guidance to the novice.

WHY HAVEN'T YOU CLEANED UP IN COMMODITIES?

Not many speculators have had the idea of cornering supplies of concrete wave-smashers. Mr. Antonio Fiducio (centre) argues that sooner or later any nation with an eroding coastline will have to come to his giant dump off Clacton. "If not," he says, "I shall sell them off as sculptures for the forecourts of trendy office blocks. They have a suggestive look which is in keeping with the spirit of the age."

I keep reading about people who make a killing in commodities and I want to get a bit of the action. How could I corner a crop?

What sort of commodities had you in mind?

Well, I don't want to buy up the nation's seed corn, or anything like that. I was brought up to despise men who cornered quinine in 'flu epidemics.

Good. Most of my clients have no such scruples.

I'd like to make my killing in something not absolutely essential to the happiness and welfare of mankind. Like ketchup.

Ketchup is a manufactured product. You would have to single out one of its vital constituents, as listed on the bottle, and go after that. Have you thought about agar, or tragacanth?

Not much.

Well, start thinking now. I assume you do not wish to take delivery of the stuff in which you deal?

Good heavens, no! All I've got is an old potting shed at the bottom of the garden. I want to make my fortune just sitting at the telephone.

Nevertheless, as you may have read in Time, *some two per cent of the traffic in commodities results in actual delivery to somebody's doorstep. It is a risk which cannot be wholly ignored. Some even go so far as to call it a nightmare.*

You mean I might come home some night and have to shovel through tons of tragacanth to get to my front door? I don't even know what the stuff looks like.

You would, after you had shovelled it for a while.

Suppose, only suppose, I decide to go for tragacanth, whatever it is. What must I do?

You buy a "future". You agree to take delivery of a load of tragacanth after a fixed period of time. If the price goes up in the meantime, you can sell your future to somebody else and take your profit. If the price falls—but let us think positively. Of course, if you want to corner the market you will have to keep on buying, and storing, and buying, and storing, until the world is desperate for tragacanth. It could cost you quite a packet.

Oh.

Basically, it is like share dealing, except that when you have a flutter in shares there's no risk of British Leyland being physically dumped on your doorstep.

There seem to be heavy risks involved. Is there no way of operating with somebody else's money?

You can buy on margin, meaning that by putting down, say, £5,000 you can buy a £100,000 future contract, and hope that somebody will take it off your hands. But the brokers will want to know something about your resources.

You mean I have to hire brokers?

Without a doubt. Have you any assets, by the way?

I have an Access card.

I may be wrong, but I do not think anyone has yet cornered an important crop, or held a nation to ransom, with no other asset than an Access card. Have you ever thought of putting your savings in a building society?

You are trying to discourage me. Obviously the whole commodity market is a carve-up by insiders. It is disgusting to think of all those scoundrels in America making a bomb out of soya beans. Why cannot I get into that game?

Those scoundrels, as you call them, had the wit to see that the mysterious disappearance of schools of Peruvian anchovies from the Pacific meant that, with anchovy meal off the market, there was no effective competitor to soya bean meal as a source of animal-feed protein.

You mean it just came to them in a flash? One minute they were telling each other dirty stories and the next they were all fighting for soya bean futures?

One or two of them read the signs and the word got around. My advice to you is to keep your ear to the ground and you may hear of the failure of a crop which will eliminate all competition for tragacanth.

I don't want to hear that word again.

Well, plumbago then. Or esparto grass.

I just don't feel happy with exotics. Right now I'm thinking of soot.

Did you say soot?

Yes, common soot. My father always said it was indispensable for killing slugs on allotments. Thanks to central heating, it now has a scarcity value. Maybe I could corner the soot supplies in south-west Surrey, just for a start.

I thought you wanted to operate ethically? If you corner soot, greenstuffs will be devoured by slugs and people will get scurvy. You can't corner soot and still have clean hands, I always say.

Oh, shut up. And good day to you.

Good day to you.

These speculators are inspecting their giant stockpile of ferrisroot, a vital substance used almost universally in the stiffening of traffic wardens' peaked caps. "Soon," says Mr. Saul Crampon (top), "the world will be beating a pathway to our door, I hope."

Resembling an Egyptian pyramid in appearance, this dump of breeze blocks near Warrington is a striking monument to the efforts of a Lancashire syndicate which hopes to force up the cost of building to heights as yet undreamed of.

The views of leading British economists are canvassed by Bernard Hollowood

K. Friedman (Univ. of Sussex)
"There is too much money about. I should make banknotes legal tender only when they have been signed and numbered—by hand and in red ink—by the Chief of the Bank of England."

Joby Bentham (Sheffield)
"The Defence of the Realm Act (DORA) should be amended to restrict shopping hours to those times when such TV programmes as Coronation Street, Match of the Day, The Big Match, Peyton Place and repeats of The Forsyte Saga are being screened."

Bill Galbraith (St. Andrew's)
"I blame the anti-smoking lobby which has diverted money from useless consumption to the inflationary purchase of foodstuffs and consumer durables. The Government should encourage people to smoke while warning them of its possible consequences."

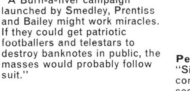

Fred Malthus (Keele)
"A Burn-a-fiver campaign launched by Smedley, Prentiss and Bailey might work miracles. If they could get patriotic footballers and telestars to destroy banknotes in public, the masses would probably follow suit."

Percy Keynes (LSE)
"Since the Government can control wages only in the public sector it is obvious that all industries and services should be nationalised immediately."

Tom Marx (Univ. of Wales)
"A return to tommy-shops (truck) might help. Sales would diminish if wages could be exchanged for goods only at specified shops situated in remote country districts, preferably in the Outer Hebrides."

Spiralling food costs are leading to an entirely fresh approach to shopping: the food co-operative. Housewives band together to buy in bulk from wholesale markets...

How to go about setting up a neighbourhood food co-operative

The first approach:
Diets are like daffodils—they taste awful. So most people are in the market for a supply of solid, nourishing food at prices they can afford. Nevertheless, like figs and persimmons, people must be handled with care. If you ask your neighbour—How would you fancy fifteen tons of assorted collard and beans for thirty bob?—he may turn shy. Try instead: "Turned out nippy again. Sort of morning you need a good cooked breakfast. Mind you, with bacon the price it is. Of course, I'm fortunate in having this friend goes down to the market, very worthwhile. I don't know if you'd be interested but, as a favour, I could ask him . . ."

Size:
Most food co-ops agree that the ideal size for a group is twelve or multiples of twelve. This is partly because it is easier to multiply by twelve than by, say, thirteen or four hundred and two. Also, much produce is distributed in dozens or multiples thereof. Leeks and ground-nuts are examples of this. You may wish to order 1 doz. assorted lean mutton carcases, a gross of nectarines, 24 mulch-grown endives or 12 cwt of nutmeg. It is most unlikely that any supplier would accept an order for 402 mulch-grown endives or that you would be able to find more than

All that is left of a West Country apple warehouse after bargain-hunting housewives from an Ottery St. Mary Food Co-operative shifted four thousand crates of Cox's Pippins in less than an hour. ▶

about a dozen people in your neighbourhood who are that keen on mulch-grown endive to begin with. On the other hand, they may like nectarines. You must judge this as best you can.

Transportation:
For twelve people, it is best to have a lorry. If the cost is shared, it need come to no more than a twelfth of what it would cost you to buy a lorry in the shops on your own. This is a further big saving. The best time to go to the markets (which open at dawn) is as early as possible—both to beat the crowds of other co-operative lorries and to get the pick of the nectarines before the rush starts. Rush can be quite palatable if it is boiled for an hour or more but it does not keep well. Avoid collard for much the same reasons. A further benefit is that people arriving by

Crisp, young endive growing in the fertile mucklands of the Busby Berkeley Food Co-operative, Staines. Housewives save up to 40p an acre. ▶

lorry are less likely to get duffed up by the market traders who are trying to squeeze out smart-alec food co-op nutters who are out to deprive them of an honest living in marketing nectarines.

Shoppers:

Two could do all the buying for twelve members, but four would be better as they could work up to twice as quickly. Whoever is talked into doing the actual shopping must be persuaded to mark down all the prices paid, otherwise it is no fun for the others to suggest where he or she went wrong. It must also be stressed that, for economic reasons, individual preferences and faddy idiosyncrasies go by the board since bulk buying is governed by the best prices available at market. If, for example, some of your members have ordered potatoes, it may turn out that mulch-grown endive is cheaper by the gross. In this case, they must get to like mulch-grown endive. If there's any argument, give them nectarines.

Distribution:

Most food co-ops use members' hall-space or loft where there is usually less furniture to move out of the way. In the growing season especially, produce like mulch-grown endive can take up a surprising amount of space. It may be necessary to charge an additional fee to cover the cost of the lorry, petrol, paper bags, clearing up blood from leaking carcases, spillage from over-ripe persimmons and the cost of clearing up after mulch-grown endive which can tread all up the stairs.

Inside the recently-enlarged larder of a terraced home at Ewell where one thrifty mum, using only her wits and an Access card, has the week-end joint for the whole neighbourhood sewn up until the turn of the century.

Just look at these advantages!

Massive savings: With the larger co-ops, it can add up to as much as one in something.

A conversation stopper: Bring the boss home to dinner and show him the 15 cwt of fresh leeks under the stairs, or a bathful of wholesale chub and barbel. Perhaps he would like to join your food co-operative.

A hedge against inflation: As prices soar, essential foodstuffs are bound to escalate in value. Figs, dates, some kinds of cabbage and chunky steaks of whale all keep well. You may be able to use your hoard as surety or collateral against a loan for a deep-freeze or garden warehouse.

Make new friends: Share an interest in finding arcane cut-price vegetables, game and grain products. Your birthday present problems solved: send him or her a bushel of bean-sprouts, a truckload of pumpkin, crates of mushrooms or a cow.

Make use of wasted space: That spare wardrobe could have a pig in, many lofts are ideal for edible fungus. Herrings can keep for weeks in a garden pool, beans and turnips thrive in a landing or hall.

This week's supply of bananas for Nos. 1-12 Sidney Street, Oldham. Said the lady at No. 8, "Bananas are full of vitamins and a bargain at this price. It's quite a novelty having them in the parlour."

YOUR SUPPER IS IN THE WINDOW BOX

by HONEYSETT

"Making the bread's easy enough—it's slicing and wrapping it that's so difficult."

"Oh, I'm sorry, I've knocked over your compost heap

"Would you care to try some of our carpet fluff wine?"

"I thought I'd practise with flies—and then get some bees."

"Yes, Friday will be fine. You'll stay to dinner, of course?"

"You don't think the cat will get jealous?"

"Well, it was raining."

"We're letting it lie fallow this year."

THE ULTIMATE ADVICE COLUMN

DON'T say we didn't warn you. Week in, week out, we City editors have been telling you how to guard against inflation. Has inflation abated? Have you listened to a blind word we've been saying? Have you, my aunt Fanny. Sometimes I wonder if it's worth it.

Let's try one more time. On these two pages you'll find everything you need to know about beating inflation. Let's go through it again carefully and this time, *do* something about it. I'm not going to tell you again.

Before we go any further, have you got any money on you? Or in the bank? You have? Well, for crying out loud! Don't you realise it's gone down to 98.7p in the £ since you started reading this? Go out now, before you read any further, and invest it. Go on.

Money

To recap—the value of money is going down faster and faster, and there's nothing the Government can do about it. Solution: everyone must invest their money in something which will appreciate in value. This means *everyone*, by the way. If just half of us do the right thing, the other half will be caught in the price and wages spiral, and we'll still have inflation. I want you *all* to put your money into something solid.

Enough talk. Time to consider your investments. Have you checked the state of the art market since you opened this copy of *Punch*? Have you been round to the estate agent today to see how house prices are going? Well, get out and do it! This isn't a reader service, you know, it's an emergency survival guide.

Liquidity

Welcome back, if you're still solvent. Now, let's take an example of the sort of person who wants to know how to beat inflation. You live in rented premises, you haven't got quite the capital to get a mortgage. Your travel and living expenses are going up faster than your income. You hesitate to plunge into the unknown world of art collecting. You shouldn't be reading a column like this in the first place and you deserve to go bankrupt.

Another example
Let's take another example. You've run up a big overdraft. You have extensive HP debts and a whacking great mortgage. You don't know where the next penny is coming from. Good! You obviously realise that if you borrow now, you will be paying back in devalued currency, and making a profit on the deal. No, I can't lend you £500, but full marks for trying.

But what about the average man in the street with only £20,000 to invest?
For this sort of medium yield type investment, I'd recommend Van Gogh Ltd. This small Belgian firm specialising in high quality canvases has, after a shaky start, produced some very good dividends and settled down to making a good profit each year. They now command an international market and are doing especially well in America. If you're looking for a slightly more risky but attractive gamble, why not try Lord Leighton Securities or Boudin Consolidated? Whatever you do, do it now and come back and read this article later.

House buying
Have you got a house? No? Then get your hands off my page—you're ruining my readership profile.

Now that *he's* gone, here's some advice for house-owners. Get a second house. Go out today and slap a deposit down on a small semi-detached villa on the fringes of Darlington or Carlisle. It's unfashionable, so it will be cheap. It's an investment, so you won't have to live there. Do it up quickly and flog it to that chap we got rid of in the first paragraph. I'll give you his address.

Who to back in the City
If you want to add to your portfolio of shares, there's still plenty of choice but for all-round performance I don't think you can do better than invest in Patrick Sergeant, City Editor of the *Daily Mail*, a consistently buoyant performer. Only last week he edited a sixteen-page Inflation Special full of doom and disaster, and turned up on page three of it, wearing a grey topper at Ascot and sounding full of the joys of summer. *That's* what I call a good performance.

Obligatory reference to German inflation in the 1920s
It couldn't happen here. On the other hand, you never know. If in doubt, I'd advise you to hedge against the complete debasement of the currency by starting a small para-military political party. There's a quite good little textbook on the subject, called *Mein Kampf*.

Quick readers
The sort of people who are going to beat inflation are shrewd investors and quick readers. The best ones will already have finished this article and be out and about beating inflation. Those of you who have only got this far should get a move on—you're five minutes behind already. The £ doesn't hang about at the same level, you know.

The beef market
Many readers have written in asking me to recommend a good fillet of steak. There's not

"One day I asked myself—what is nobody else collecting?"

much choice here, but I can recommend a small flutter on $\frac{1}{2}$ lb. best Scotch from a small butcher in south Oxford, whose name I will supply on receipt of a small fee. It should appreciate 10% within 24 hours—then resell.

State of the fine art market

All the good stuff has been cornered long ago, of course, but there is still scope in some of the fringe areas of the art world. Here's a quick guide to the market movement.

Victorian school furniture	rising steadily
Union Jack tea-trays	level
Slightly chipped Edward VIII mugs	rising steadily
Pre-motorway road maps	rising steadily
Caricatures of Harold Wilson	recovering after bad fall
Old Times/Sotheby indexes	spectacular gains

No, I do not own any shares in Patrick Sergeant

It's often cynically assumed that when a City Editor like me tips a share or commodity, he himself has invested in it or at the very least been prompted in some way. (This is only true of ex-City editors.) For instance, it might be thought that because I advised you to back Patrick Sergeant, I had some interest in him. Nothing could be further from the truth. A City Editor simply cannot afford to be connected in any way with the world of finance.

. . . Patrick! You're looking well. Did you have a nice time at Ascot? Yes, I managed to get that plug in. What are you drinking?

Book-buying
The recent fantastic surge in book prices has come as a severe blow to those ordinary people who are not yet owner/readers, but are still renting their reading matter from libraries. Some of them may now find outright ownership of their very own book beyond their means, especially if they have set their sights on something substantial set in its own cover and dust jacket. They would be well advised to aim lower and hope to get a council paperback.

How do I set about becoming a currency speculator, asset-stripper and all-round quick profiteer and no questions asked?
I don't quite understand this query. Do you mean you are *not* already a currency speculator, asset-stripper or fly-by-night capitalist? Then why are you reading this column? If you are really serious, join one of the better schools for correspondence capitalism. Apply to the Stock Exchange, London, enclosing an S.A.E. and mentioning my name.

Quick growth high yield super whiteness sex appeal
If all else fails, sell your car number plate. There is bound to be someone in the phone book with the same initials as your car.

An apology
It has been drawn to our attention that our humorous references to Patrick Sergeant could be taken to imply that he was in some way connected with the preparation of this Beat Inflation Guide. We now recognise that there is absolutely no truth in any suggestion of any kind whatsoever. Sorry, Patrick. What are you drinking?

End on a cheerful note
Whatever our temporary difficulties . . . market basically sound . . . taking longer to recover than we thought . . . boom in the autumn . . . devaluation scares . . . hidden assets . . . there'll always be an England. . . .

SEE WHAT THE BOYS IN THE BACK ROOM WILL BUY

DAVID WILLIAMS speculates on the junk boom

ESTATE-AGENTS would call my place a residence. It's tatty, but definitely not bijou. This I say in no boastful spirit, but simply to explain the spare room. I think of this now as a sort of Yukon: an unheated rubbish-dump for years, and then suddenly, almost before you know, there's gold in them there throw-outs and bygones. Don't ever tell me inflation benefits nobody. It benefits a hoarder.

I've always been a compulsive keeper of things, and this spare room, being big, has been an encouragement. Visitors, peeping in at it, draw in their breath with a hiss. Crossing it diagonally is like scrambling in the Dolomites; you probe each foothold ahead for safety and watch out for lethal falls of leather hat-boxes and Charles Dickens in 30 volumes illustrated in half calf.

I have the *Zeitschrift der Naturwissenschaftlicher Erforschung* in there, strung up in piles of 12 and dating from January 1897. I have a pair of button-boots worn by my mother when attending, in a kerbstone capacity, the coronation of George V. There are three dozen pairs of Bavarian braces, baroque and decorative almost to decadence. I *had* thousands of cigarette cards, including a set of fifty Allied Army Generals—of World War One, not Two—most of them wearing bushy moustaches and trying to look like Kitchener only not quite so nasty.

Mention ought also to be made of a handloom of my wife's measuring five feet by four which could probably still be made to work although it got knocked about a bit by the Luddites of 1816. High up on top of a vast Victorian wardrobe decorated with mahogany grapes, stands a rococo samovar. This my grandmother claimed to have wheedled out of Anton Chekhov as he sharpened his axe in readiness for laying about him in his cherry orchard. A very tall-boy holds my collection of German beer-mats which laid side by side would, my computer tells me, weave a circle round the Albert Hall.

Over the years I've had to fight to preserve this private limbo. When it comes to dust women will never settle for letting the stuff settle. I have been made use of, too, and this brings in my brother-in-law, who stops over for a night with us every six months or so, producing anxiety as another might a bottle of Algerian plonk. He does a roaring trade in general dealing, much of it with stately homes intent upon keeping up with the Longleats in the safari park business. All one Wednesday will find him in the Matto Grosso; the following Saturday he'll be dining at the Marquess of where-ever's Tudor incubus and driving a hard bargain over a stoppered carboy full of piranha fish and picked bones. On his last visit he was carrying a torpid rattlesnake in a cage. I hung about at some distance until, to humour me, he said he'd put it in the spare room.

At three next morning, the night having turned suddenly warm, I woke to the sound of grunts, bangs and slitherings from below. I rushed down. My brother-in-law in gaudy pyjamas, and electric torch in one hand and a forked stick in the other, was climbing about the spare room raising dust and lunging at an invisible yet militant rattle. He emerged after a minute, holding his writhing merchandise between finger and thumb just below the business, or spitting, end.

It was worth fifteen guineas an inch to the Duke of Somewhere, he told me, who was turning his master-bedroom into a reptile house. Smudged but nonchalant, he said the sudden warm spell must have livened it up, and God, what a tip I had in there, and couldn't I do something about it?

I said, "What sort of something?" and he said, "Leave it with me," and that was the start of it all. My spare room is thinning out. I'm laying down 1959 clarets in the cellar and studying the brochures for the next round-the-world, chase-the-sunshine cruise on the *Chimborazo*, where the calorie-intake per caput per meal is high enough to make a cardiologist whinny. I also have a new Bismark 3500 which will do four miles an hour in top and against which the dealer made a generous allowance in respect of my Sunbeam bicycle with chain-guard and Sturmey-Archer three-speed, a machine which had fought for the right of way with hansom cabs and hadn't missed highwaymen by all that much.

It was during the week after the rattlesnake had squirmed amuck that my brother-in-law rang back to say hadn't he seen some cigarette cards in there? I said thousands, mentioning in particular the fifty Allied Army Generals of World War One. Hoarsely he asked whether they were in mint condition. I said General Nivelle's moustache was still glossy, and Marshal Foch could have been lying holed up in an unopened packet of Gold Flake for upwards of half a century, so untouched by time he seemed. Trying to keep a tremor out of his contralto, he asked had I been down to a certain St. James's Square auctioneers, and what else had I got? I said No, and would he care to take a shufti?

It wasn't of course possible to get the door fully open but he got his head round and remained rigid in a corkscrew position for so long I thought rigor mortis might have set in. I tweaked. He re-emerged. He said his eyes dazzled. I was to form a company out of myself pronto (Disposals Ltd.), and get down to St. James's on my Sunbeam taking with me two fifty-sets of cigarette-cards. No more because any sort of mass unloading would give the market an irrecoverable shock. He had felt like Lord Carnarvon and Howard Carter when they'd first lighted up their carbide lamps in Tutankhamun's tomb in 1922, and I wasn't to lie awake worrying about inflation any more, not at any rate till around the 1990s by when the whole bloody set-up would have become hopeless or just hilarious anyway according to how you looked at it. His commission would be five per cent, he said, and in his excitement left without a potto commissioned by a belted earl.

The auctioneers keep sending round an imploring bowler-hatted man to say they're ready to call at any time, with their special pantechnicon which is foam padded on the inside, for my Victorian wardrobe with the mahogany grapes. But on this I'm standing firm. I still need storage-space.

"*Back to nature! See how the resourceful cave dweller provides meat for his family.*"

"*He was lucky—another stockbroker broke **his** fall.*"

The Government and the Building Societies want to make things easier for young home buyers. And with ever-lengthening mortgage terms, the would-be buyers are getting younger and younger...

The Punch
Equitable Building
Society

Patron: Rupert Bear

Whereas it is more or less understood between both parties in writing, picture-books, illustrative blocks, friezes or an abacus, that the would-be borrower from the Society treasure chest, or assets, hereinafter deemed only to include such persons of a proven tidiness and good husbandry over such properties as they may now hold, be they forts, wigwams, garaging or Wendy developments, and who may moreover be deemed likely to pay sufficient attention in their study as to be expected to land a steady job with prospects in the years which shall accrue from their current age of seven years or less, are proven nevertheless unlikely to see their way to a two-up, two-down terrace in suburbia of grown-up proportions before such time as they may be old and dead, excepting that an undertaking be entered into in good time. The Society shall make available the resources of THE NURSERY PLAN, for which it is laid down that the minimum first investment shall be of the value of one conker, or its equivalent in Corgi toys, Meccano or sweetmeats and confectionery. NOW THEREFORE the plan shall become convertible, upon maturity, into a Proposal, Indemnification and Declaration of good intent at such time when the borrower's command of English may be trusted, together with the Passbook, Badges, Bicycle Stickers and all other properties of The Society, together with The Holy Bible and a blank cheque attached thereto, which shall be surrendered to The Society for an indefinite term as an irrevocable contract, as of slavery, for an indefinite term and together with any increase, multiplication, increment or aggrandisement of the agreed sum, howsoever apparently fixed, which may necessitate the passing of the outstanding capital debt even unto the next generation. The Society will undertake, like as not, to provide a mortgage against the purchase of an approved property or dwelling, depending on how things go.

How to stay rich though British

by THELWELL

*"I've been thinking about this Government re-training scheme, love. Do you
fancy being a welder?"*

"Any jobs going, mate?"

*"I think we ought to hang on
to him—beef's bound to go up."*

"If I can get the old couple out of the boot. I'll give you first refusal."

*"I expect about six houses to the acre
—how about you?"*

"I'd like him to have the opportunities I missed.
We're hoping to get him down the mines."

"Charles decided to lay it
down as an investm. . . ."

Dieticians have recently discovered that many of the foods which are reputedly good for health and conducive to slimmer, more beautiful bodies, actually contain harmful **high prices.** A fillet steak, for instance, which is low on calories and high on protein, undoes all its good work by its enormous content of **aggregate cost** (a technical term for the loss of £s involved). It may even render the eater unable to have another good meal for 24 hours.

Another alarming discovery is that many hitherto reputable foods are subject to **reduced availability.** This is a highly complicated scientific concept, but roughly it means that if **Vogue** recommended all its readers to eat quail to make their cheeks soft, and all the readers took the advice, the quail would become extinct overnight. As any ecologist will tell you, this would alter the shape of the Scottish landscape radically, as well as make the ptarmigan feel nervous.

The answer we have devised is quite simple. Eat foods which are low on **income damage.** Choose dishes which have a maximum **re-use value.** That way you will be able to eat as much as you like—as long as you keep strictly to this seven-day diet chart! (To begin with, many of you will find it difficult to restrict yourselves to **cost-free** foods. You're bound to lapse now and again, but persevere; the temptation to change a pound note will soon vanish. Remember, it's always better to save than slim.)

THE PUNCH DIET SHEET

For those
who can't afford
to eat

DAY 1
breakfast
half a grapefruit
small cup of coffee
Any type of grapefruit would do, but the best kind is the one that rolls by accident off the greengrocer's stall into your shopping bag. Eat the segments, but do not squeeze. *No sugar and milk in your coffee.* Sugar and milk are full of dangerous *cost escalation.*
lunch
half a grapefruit
small cup of coffee
The other half of breakfast's grapefruit—again do not squeeze. For a change, try your cup of coffee iced. This avoids harmful hidden *heating charges.*
dinner
grapefruit juice
snoek and knödel pie
cheese

Squeeze the two grapefruit halves left over from breakfast and lunch. Snoek and knödel pie is cooked in exactly the same way as steak and kidney pie, except that snoek is used instead of steak and knödel instead of kidneys. Knödel are German dumplings, which are made by letting lumps of pastry fall into the pie. This dish is traditionally eaten with the fingers, which avoids unnecessary *cutlery investment.* For cheese, why not try one of the wide range of English offerings such as mouse-trap (available in most good mouse-traps)?

DAY 2
breakfast
Scottish rarebit
small cup of coffee
Scottish rarebit is a variant of the more familiar Welsh rarebit, made with dust instead of cheese. Just pop a piece of

toast under the grill for a moment and it's ready.

lunch
oeuf cuit a l'eau bouillant
A satisfying French regional dish, made by leaving an egg in boiling water for four minutes. If this is too rich for your taste, leave the egg for dinner and skip lunch.

supper
hard-boiled egg
scrag end of loaf
For the main dish, ask your baker to carve you off a crusty joint—the so-called Door-Step. It can be toasted, grilled or barbecued; whichever way you prepare it, these lesser-known cuts have unexpected *investment value*.

DAY 3
breakfast
nothing
lunch
nothing
dinner
crab ramekins
gigot d'agneau, with carrots, artichokes and salsify
syllabub
choice of seven cheeses
brandy
The best recipe for this deeply satisfying meal is being invited out to dinner. If you have it at home it is not at all satisfying— try half a grapefruit for a change.

DAY 4
breakfast
roast half of grapefruit
champignon sur pain grillé
The mushroom dish, a perennial favourite with impoverished old ladies in Provence, consists of a single mushroom diced and lightly fried in its own dripping, placed on a soupçon of toast.
lunch
mackerel, Viennese style
The Viennese do not like mackerel. Sensibly, they much prefer the cheaper cuts of whitebait.
dinner
potage mackerel, Viennese style
casserole de potage mackerel, Viennese style
bread et marge pudding

DAY 5
breakfast
oeuf sans saucisse, lard, tomate et champignons
lunch
pensioner's rabbit pie
Pensioners have traditionally found rabbit too rich a dish, and have long preferred to replace it with hamster which can be obtained free from any pet shop or primary school. Is traditionally served with no vegetables.
dinner
rolled joint
Obtainable locally

DAY 6
breakfast
cocktail de supreme de left-over de grapefruit
toast a la maison
lunch
veal escalope milanese a la muggeridge
The celebrated chef Muggeridge based this recipe on a report in some newspaper or other that calves received unutterably cruel treatment while in transit from Rouen to Marseille, and deleted the veal element from the dish. It remains a classic of the *cost-free* pasta school.
dinner
whelk cocktail
lapin bourguignon
crab apple fool

DAY 7
breakfast
large cup of coffee
lunch
viande et deux legumes
A classic French dish based on an old meat and vegetable recipe. Nowadays it takes the form of sauté left-over plus left-overs, though this is usually dropped in favour of a ham sandwich *à la luncheon voucher*.
dinner
lettuce vinaigrette
blackbird pie
zabaglione (optional: to be refused)

SLIMMING GUIDE FOR PETS

If food shortages and inflation mean that we have to make do with less, that means all of us—pets included . . .

JUST THINK! By getting your pet down to his proper weight (see our Pet's-Weight-At-A-Glance Chart) you can not only make sure he is enjoying full health, but also spare some of the world's food for those starving elsewhere. An underfed pariah dog in India, for instance, or a needy hamster in an African school, many of whom desperately need such educational tools as budgie seed and lettuce for rabbits.

So why not get your pet slimming today! We have devised an easy-to-learn crash fortnight diet which can get your pet looking his old best again—and he'll enjoy it! No stick insect likes looking fat and bumpy; no mouse wants to lie in a corner when he could be out and about with his treadmill. *You've* all had the fun of shedding extra pounds; let *them* know what it's like to throw off the milligrams! And they'll have the added satisfaction of knowing that they're saving an Asian goldfish's life.

A fortnight's crash diet for pets

Day 1
Biscuit and water. No sugar lumps, chocolate or other delicacy. Some pets should never have sugar lumps anyway; an angel fish, for instance, can easily be stunned by one thrown carelessly in a tank.

Days 2 & 3
As Day 1. After three days the average pet will be cleaned of the impurities in his system, and showing a new bodily vigour. A budgie will show this, for instance, by busily pecking his mirror; an Alsatian by biting a piece out of his master. Encourage them by patting and stroking them frequently, or have a friendly wrestle with your python.

Day 4
By now your pet will be ravenously hungry. This shows itself in various ways. A Shetland pony will eat your jersey; a tortoise will go to sleep for three months. So it's time to give him a little bit of solid food, but fresh and healthy. A bit of fish for your cat, perhaps, a bit of cat for your baby hawk, some bush for your hawkmoth, or even catfish for your bush baby—the variations are endless.

Days 5 & 6
Keep him to half rations for another two days. By the way, don't worry if you have a Mayfly as a pet and he hasn't moved since Day Two. He is dead. This is quite normal.

Days 7 & 8
If your pet is carnivorous, add some green stuff to his diet now. If he is herbivorous, feed him to your carnivore. If you have a vegetarian carnivore, write about it to one of the tabloid dailies and get some money for an amusing letter.

Day 9

By now, your pet should be nearly down to the right weight and sporting a glistening, sleek coat, unless he is a tortoise. If he *is* a tortoise and sporting a glistening, sleek coat, the cat is sitting on him.

Days 10, 11 & 12

Notice that we have avoided so far any tinned, frozen or pre-cooked foods, which are not only expensive but don't taste as good as fresh food, and a pet who doesn't look forward to mealtime will not become lean and graceful, and have his photo in *Vogue*.

Days 13 & 14

Your pet is now fit and well again, and you have saved a lot of money. Go back to Day One.

Today's doggy exercise

1 Up, down and together . . .

2 Up, down and together . . .

3 Up, down and—oops!

How to weigh your pet

SOME PETS can easily be weighed—a turtle or stick insect can just be popped on the scales and measured, though in the latter case no weight will be registered. Many animals are rather trickier, though; here are some tips on the most common.

Monkeys

No use trying to get a monkey to stay on the ordinary bathroom scales. It's much more effective to buy a spring balance and get him to hang from it.

Birds

Weigh the cage with the bird in, then weigh it again with the bird out. The difference between the two figures is the weight of the

CONTINUED ON NEXT PAGE

bird. If there is no difference, the bird was airborne first time round.

Snakes

As few people have more than two or three bathroom scales to put together in a row, this is a tricky one; weighing snakes section by section is inaccurate, even if you carefully mark metre lengths in yellow pencil. Best if possible to gorge them with a small mammal, previously weighed, get them comatose and then curl them up neatly in a basket and pop them on the scales. Remember, $S = W - (B + PWM + AOBOF)$, where S is the snake, B is the basket, W the total weight, PWM the previously weighed mammal and AOBOF any odd bits of fluff.

Dogs

Most dogs are quite easy, but the bigger sort always leave one leg dangling off the edge. Slip a small weighing machine in their basket, and read off the weight when they are asleep on top of it at night. NB. Boxers are traditionally weighed with shorts on, snarling at their opponent.

Hedgehogs

Gloves should be worn, though it takes ages to get gloves on to hedgehogs.

Chihuahua

Slip a chihuahua into your pocket and stand on the machine. Then weigh yourself without. Be careful not to stand on the chihuahua. They are very savage and can inflict terrible damage on shoelaces.

Woodworm

Only possible to weigh if you knew the weight of your furniture beforehand.

Nervous Ticks

Virtually impossible to weigh.

BEFORE: Prince Lamb Chop III, starting our fortnight crash diet.

AFTER: The new, slim youthful animal after the course.

YOUR PETS'-WEIGHT-AT-A-GLANCE CHART

These weights are only approximate and allowance should be made for a young or unusually big pet. The ideal weight for some Arctic pets fluctuates wildly from summer to winter. Very occasionally freak weights are encountered; one parrot which was measured at fifteen stone three turned out to specialise in imitations of Peter Ustinov.

PET	IDEAL WEIGHT
Angel Fish	½ oz
Goldfish	2 oz (Troy wt.)
Mackerel	60p per lb
Hamster	3 oz
Tadpole	4 oz per 1,000
French poodle	1 kilo
Sea Horse	½ hand
Snake	2 lbs per foot
Frog	10 lbs per sq in (take-off thrust)
Lemming	120 ft per sec per sec
Turtle	3 lbs
Mock Turtle	12 oz net plus salt, pepper, spices and permitted colouring

THE BEST THINGS IN LIFE ARE FREE

or, rather, says VINCENT MULCHRONE, the free things in life are best

WHEN the Indonesian Embassy threw a splendid party at the London Hilton, they actually allowed for one hundred and fifty "uninvited guests". Freeloaders.

Practical, charming and fatalistic, they had cottoned on to the fact that the British will go to extraordinary lengths in pursuit of free booze, food, or rubbing shoulders with the mighty. To their surprise, only about ninety-five freeloaders turned up. Said the Embassy: "It must be the holidays."

Very civilised, the Indonesians. Given that even freeloaders must take a holiday sometime, they had gone too far in laying off the diplomatic bet that freeloaders might account for a good quarter of the Ambassador's entertaining fund. They were working on the experience of the Nepalese Embassy which, in 1969, gave a party for one hundred people. Came the night, one hundred and ninety-five turned up and drank them dry in less than forty minutes. An embarrassed Nepalese is almost indistinguishable from an unembarrassed Nepalese. But they learned another lesson about how low the Sahibs have sunk that night.

The next day, the secret army of freeloaders got their first, official recognition from the Foreign Office which said, in a pained voice, "The trouble is that foreign embassies don't like to demand invitations at the door. We feel the Diplomatic Corps should sort it out themselves." In fact, the current spate of security has more or less sorted it out for them. God's gift to freeloaders, any nation's national day celebrations (from Albania on November 28 to Zambia on October 24), aren't what they were. (God's writ never ran at the Soviet Embassy, where they never had the least compunction in demanding to see your invitation card, and even checking it against a numbered list.)

It is difficult to define the median freeloader. He must be uninvited, of course. He must get in where he's not wanted. He must consume food and drink not intended for him. And he might, as a sort of grace note, hobnob with people he persuades to accept him as an equal.

110

Purists might object, but I would extend the definition to those people who insinuate themselves into subsidised works canteens and get themselves a damned good lunch for 35p. It's not exactly free, but at least they're getting a cheap meal intended for somebody else in a place where they've no right to be.

It's getting away with it that counts among people known as "jibbers". Back in the late 50s a young chap made it his hobby to attend almost every big party (because the bigger they are, the easier they are to crash) attended by Princess Alexandra. He'd no particular crush on her. He just liked having her around. And *he* was a porter at Euston station. Any class of person can play. In the 20s it was young bucks crashing debs' parties. Oddly enough, the actress Mrs. Patrick Campbell was a prodigious freeloader. Challenged by her non-host, so to speak, at a party in New York, she said: "I am Mrs. Patrick Campbell, and your flies are undone." She was deep into his champagne before he had recovered his composure.

That cheeky chappie, Max Miller, used to indulge in a fairly innocent form of freeloading when he was king of the Moss Empire circuit. Two minutes before the interval he would station himself at the circle bar with a large glass of tonic water into which his fans fairly queued to pour large gins.

But we are drifting away from serious freeloading, best practised in the capital, because that's where all the embassies are. As new nations proliferate, so do the number of national days and the foreigner has come to the conclusion that the best way to make his mark in Britain is to open the Embassy door, jump back, the way they do at sales, and watch the British get sloshed. Embassy receptions are the easiest mark and the easiest of all are the, well, coloured Embassies, still nervous about slinging white men down the Embassy steps in case they're accused of operating a colour bar. The Indians and Pakistanis are particularly susceptible, because they try to out-do each other in numbers, wherein, for the freeloader, lies safety. I shall not break the jibbers' code by giving you their dates. They're easily looked up, anyway. What I will reveal is the *modus operandi*.

I'm taking it that you have the right clothes and supercilious bearing. Next you need a highly embossed visiting card, which might go something like:

M. Vincent Mulchrone, K-G a A, B.C., Dott. Ing., I.C.U.

The initials stand for Kommandit-Gesellschaft auf Aktien (or a private company partly owned as a joint stock company), British Columbia, Dottore in Ingegneria (Doctor of Engineering), and International Communications Union.

You can perm millions of these combinations from the pages of the *International Year Book and Statesmen's Who's Who*, available at your friendly neighbourhood library. Place the card before the flustered official at the desk, look over his shoulder at the throng and shout "Ah, Francois! Ça va, mon pot?" and streak for the bar. Some of the more sophisticated embassies in London have collections of these cards, which they preserve in rueful admiration.

This sort of freeloading was almost kid's stuff until 1968, when the American Embassy decided to work a flanker and switched its Fourth of July reception from the evening to noon, when most of its freeloaders were presumably tied up in the sewers of Bermondsey or at their desks in the Min of Ag. For, as an American Embassy spokesman said, "How's the butler to know when someone arrives and says he's the High Commissioner for somewhere . . .?" Their example was quickly followed, first by the Hungarians, then the Czechs, then—but, again, I think you should in all decency find out for yourself.

Trouble is, the embassies have gone quite crazy about security these days, and the ancient and honourable practice of jibbing has fallen on hard times. In this century, the Press was tut-tutting about freeloaders as far back as 1909, saying they were well known in society but without actually risking a writ by naming them. More recently the well known society hostess (well, that's what it says) Mrs. Bunty Kinsman had a stranger walk into a party, pocket a bottle of Scotch from the sideboard, and walk out again. That she did nothing about it is partly explained by the fact that she was throwing a fancy dress party, and she was bemused by the guest (or was he a freeloader of exceptional talent?), who turned up entirely swathed in bandages as The Invisible Man.

It's not an exclusively British trait, of course. It's on record that, in 1966, the wife of the Finnish Ambassador to Rome came across six women shovelling caviare, smoked salmon and reindeer steaks into big plastic bags from her smorgasbord table. She got rid of them. But when the Swedish Ambassador arrived, there was no food left. And you wonder how diplomatic incidents begin?

But in spite of security at embassies, and hawk-eyed hostesses, the addicted freeloader still has plenty of room for manoeuvre. Go to any big hotel at 1.15 pm and note from the displayed list at least two of the several receptions currently in swing. Watch your timing. They usually start at 12.30. By 1.15 pm the secretary, missing all the fun because she has to take names at the door, will have been slipped three gins by the young executive who is trying to gain her favours on the cheap. By 1.15 pm they'll be so deep into the company's booze and buffet that you'll never be noticed. If you *are*, you say, "I thought I didn't recognise anybody. I'm supposed to be at the Silkworm Society's reception." They'll probably think it very funny and press another drink on you before pointing you towards the other reception where, with a bit of aplomb, you can repeat the performance.

Big weddings are a pushover because all you are asked, by groomsmen overawed by their temporary office, is "Bride or groom?" Take a quick shufti down the nave, and choose the bigger party. Somebody's sure to give you a lift to the reception. The suggestion of a tear at the thought that young Cynthia, whom you've known since she was so high, will stop any awkward questions. *They'll* think you're one of *hers*, and *they'll* think you're one of *his*. Nothing to it.

I can also reveal, for obvious reasons, that some of the best freeloading in the capital is done from 4 pm every Wednesday at the Dorchester and the Waldorf Hotels where, respectively, Littlewoods and Vernons unveil their giant pools winner of the week.

I well remember—well, I half remember—the night when this French waiter ("More champagne? Certainlee, m'sieur"), looked at his watch at 9 pm and said to four dedicated reporters, in pure Bermondsey, "Ain't you got no bleedin' 'omes to go to?"

The pools people are very generous with their hospitality, but experience has given them a keen eye for the freeloader. You could try turning up wearing a flat cap and shouting, "Ahm 'is brother," but I wouldn't advise it. They have ways of making you leave.

It's just silly old me, I know, but my favourite freeloader didn't actually qualify as a jibber on account of the fact that she was a barmaid in Chelsea who lived in. She had a lover who, every night, brought her a single rose, which she would take to bed in a tumbler of water. The landlord was deeply touched until, one night, he smelled the rose. The whiff he got was not from the flower but from the water. Which was gin.

Pity about that. If you run into her at some reception, say hello from the rest of us jibbers.

...and this little piggy spent it all

Safety last with GRAHAM

"Just what I say—where's the incentive to save?"

"Now isn't this nicer than buying stuffy old National Savings Certificates?"

"If I put into British Savings Bonds, will that
Mr. Healey get his hands on it?"

"You and your little nest-egg!"

"It's a pity there isn't a Save-As-You-Loaf scheme."

"I started from nothing, worked hard, scrimping and saving, a little here, a little there, till I had the good luck to win this fortune on the pools."

"Why not give fivers a rest, Sid, and do us a nice endowment policy?"

"It's Tom's form of compulsory saving."

A RAND
IN THE HAND

by William Hardcastle

EACH winter brings its challenge. In the power-cut dark days of 1972/73 the hot commodities were candles and camping gas. Last winter it was petrol; do you remember how you queued for an hour for a gallon and a half? We are now advised that these discomforts are mere pinpricks compared to the punishment that is to come. Hyper-inflation is the name of the horror ahead, and the smart people are already working on ways to survive it.

A book called *You Can Profit from a Monetary Crisis* is already Number Four on the best-seller lists in America. It is strong on gold, and so is that wise whizz-kid of the City of London, Mr. Jim Slater, who—and only half in fun—has already worked out his own hyper-inflation survival kit.

His advice is to buy as many Krugerrands as you can manage. KRs are a gold coin which they have started minting in South Africa and which can be legally purchased in this country for £80 a time. They are of a handy size so that you can carry quite a few around in your waistcoat pockets or in a money belt round your middle. According to Mr. Slater, when hyper-inflation hits they will constitute a currency that will keep its head while all around are losing theirs.

Up to now, of course, the pound is only mildly dotty. So far inflation is running at a mere 20 per cent. What happens when a currency goes stark staring mad may be witnessed currently in Chile, which at last reckoning was experiencing an annual rate of inflation of 746.2 per cent. Based on the value of the *escudo* only a few years ago, a bus ride in Santiago now costs £10, a newspaper £15, and a salami sandwich around £25. That's hyper-inflation, folks, and there are those who say it could happen here.

As the possessor of a persistent peasant mentality I don't normally get too worked up over the gloomier profundities of our economic and financial experts. As often as not I just don't understand them. But I must admit that I was somewhat disturbed when I talked to the editor of a leading financial newspaper the other day. I asked him what he'd invest his money in now that the stock market was in such soggy shape. "Corned beef," was his crisp reply. Mr. Jim Slater prefers sardines, still a relatively cheap, long-lasting and easily-stored form of protein. I imagine Mr. Slater must make quite a noise as he walks, his sardine cans rattling against his Krugerrands.

Except that, when the time comes, he won't walk—he'll be riding a bike. That is the third item in the Slater hyper-inflation survival kit. The thinking, of course, is that petrol will become prohibitively expensive, the nation will not be able to afford to buy it, so pedal-power will be the answer. But has Mr. Slater thought deeply enough? I am reminded that inner tubes matched Hershey chocolate bars and Lucky Strike cigarettes as the main items of currency in the post-war German black market. So pack a couple of spares in your saddlebag, Jim.

That is the main point about hyper-inflation. Money goes out of style. It gets so funny that it laughs itself out of court. The fourth item in Slater's survival kit is a rather sombre one. A machine gun. The theory is that Latin American-style inflation could lead to Latin American-style revolution. The thought of Mr. Slater at the last ditch makes a grim picture. Weighed down with gold coins and sardines, and both tires punctured, he rests his gun on the handlebars and . . .

But he's not a man to be jeered at. While I've been sitting around all these years, financially speaking just twiddling my thumbs, Mr. Slater has been making six different fortunes. If I'd followed his example ten years ago I would be up to my earlobes in Krugerrands by now. I'm the sort of sucker who buys a set of silver Churchill medallions for £16.50 only to find their metal value is a mere £4.50. So his advice, however jokingly intended, must be heeded. But what should a Hardcastle hyper-inflation survival kit consist of?

Food and warmth—those are the necessities. That suggests a return to my native North-East where you can pick sea coal off the beach. It takes some drying off, but it works. The central heating system would, of course, be scrapped but the oil tank could be used to store Newcastle Brown Ale. It would not last forever but seven hundred gallons of Geordie Infuriator would go quite a long way.

The poaching possibilities up there are considerable. Salmon take no heed of monetary crises. Fiddle under the rocks at low tide with a golf iron and you can catch quite a few crabs. Chemical fertilisers imported from abroad might soon become prohibitive but that would mean that fields would return to their primitive state and wild mushrooms would begin to flourish once more. So pick a few mushrooms, poach a salmon, catch a crab, and sip an aperitif of brown ale while they're cooking on the sea-coal fire. It would be an idyllic life, and to hell with the retail price index.

I can't make up my mind about a bicycle. I never could mend a puncture properly. The little rubber patches would fail to stick even when I did manage to spot the leak in a bucket of water. I also had the devil of a time getting the tire back on the rim again. Perhaps I could find a model with hard tires, and the shaking would do my liver good. Nor am I keen on fire-arms, if only for my own safety. I think I'd settle for one of those all-purpose schoolboy's knives which would take nails out of tires as well as horses' hooves. As for sardines, I can't stand them, though we must remember that in a state of hyper-inflation goods become money and money is the stuff you paper the wall with. Hyper-inflation might cast the money changers out of the temple but their place would soon be taken by an equivalent number of sardine sellers, and I'd be in there bartering my brislings for a pot of shrimp paste along with the best of them.

I am making it sound as if I'm a very efficient fellow, a provident sort in the Slater style. Alas, this is not the case. I feel sure that even if I had the foresight to stock up on sardines I'd lose the can opener. If I started to collect Krugerrands I'd leave them in the suit that went to the cleaners yesterday. I'm just not the survival kit type, I'm afraid, so I suppose I'll just continue praying to the new national patron saint—St. Micawber.

START YOUR OWN CURRENCY

**Distrust the pound?
Afraid of the dollar?
Play safe—set up your own
system in opposition to sterling.
Here are five currencies already
in the exchange market . . .**

Penny Black Cube

Postage stamps have long been used as pieces of barter, but the very fact that to preserve their value they must not be handled has worked against their use as currency. Now ingeniously embedded in small plastic cubes, the Penny Black has taken its rightful place as a valid denomination. Useful for buying Chelsea meals, Habitat furniture, Casa Pupo rugs and country weekends, though it may have to be changed through sterling sometimes. At the moment the Penny Black Cube is worth about 3 Betjemans or 5 Cup Final Tickets (see Tickets).

Tickets

A wildly fluctuating currency. Despite the disappointment of some of the colourful denominations (the Callas Revival collapsed spectacularly some time ago, and the Cup Final Ticket, once impregnable, has been sinking slowly for several years), speculators never lose faith in it. Ones to buy at the moment are Turner Exhibition Private Views and Jesus Christ Superstar. On the whole, avoid the Wimbledon 75 issue, which may turn out to be worthless.

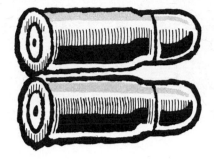

House

The single largest currency at present on the market, it has risen against the £ in an astonishing manner. Perhaps its greatest asset is that it is the only known piece of exchange yet invented which you can live in. As one House is so expensive as to be beyond the means of most speculators, special arrangements can be made for you to live in it while you are still buying it. There is one terrible snag, however. If you should ever wish to realise your investment, you immediately have to buy another House.

Ammo

An interesting regional development from Northern Ireland, this fully developed currency ranges right from the low value Bullet to the Mortar and even the much-prized Rocket Launcher (5,000 Bullets = 1 Rocket Launcher). Its main disadvantage is that it is very hard to convert into sterling, though easily bought for Czech or Polish currency. In some parts of Ulster they use little else. Efforts to make it catch on here are being made at the moment, though not with all that much success so far.

Bond Street Medallions

Not unlike our own sterling, Bond Street Medallions are a form of coinage in which 5 Betjemans = 1 Anniversary, 10 Anniversaries = 1 Churchill, 4 Churchills = 1 Royal. Once tied to the £, it was cut free a few years ago and the Churchill now floats. It has increased fairly satisfactorily in value, though there are still difficulties. The lowest denomination, the Betjeman, is worth more than £1, which means problems with change; it's still impossible to get a cup of tea with it, for example. Until they create a very small coin (a Parkinson Guest? a Milligan Poem?) it will never rival sterling.

ONE DAY MY PRINTS WILL COME

LIKE you, I have been worrying about this wealth tax. My problem is not just how they're going to value my Vermeers and my two-year-olds, my Charles Heidsieck '66 and my de Lamerie mustard-pots, though that's going to be difficult enough as it is because the mere threat of the tax will have ruined all the bona fide markets. And in whatever way they decide to value my country estates I shall only be able to pay the tax by cutting off the north-east corner of the paddock and pushing it along in a wheelbarrow to Mr. Denis Healey's room at the Treasury.

No; what's really concerning me is the new problem presented by my photograph albums and how they're going to be assessed for tax. Let me explain. I see that a volume of 94 Victorian photographs taken by Mrs. Julia Margaret Cameron has been sold at Sotheby's to a Mr. Sam Wagstaff of New York for no less a sum than £52,000. The vogue for old photographs seems to be growing, though values of course vary. Not every photographer is a Mrs. Cameron. Nevertheless, some twenty snaps of the slums of Glasgow taken in 1870 by a Mr. Thomas Annan recently fetched £3,600 and I reckon that's pretty good going even for the City Hall let alone for sombre close-ups of the Gorbals.

As the Treasury is bound to realise in due course that my own photographic work is of outstanding distinction, I am interested to discover how Sotheby's managed to whip up these remarkable prices. I don't think it can have been just the technical quality of Mrs. Cameron's compositions because even in 1863 her work was described as "blurred"; and a waspish letter from Mrs. C., defending her style with many telling points about the legitimacy of focus, itself fetched £2,000.

For his part, Mr. Annan is referred to as "a master of chiaroscuro" though we must, in all conscience, note that the art critic of the *Glasgow Herald* rather brusquely described the prints as fuzzy.

120

I find all this most interesting. So, eventually, will the Treasury. My own view of Cromer Pier taken with a Number 2 Box Brownie in the summer of 1924 has, like Mr. Annan's work, been the subject of mixed acclaim. I am, however, obviously now entitled to describe as chiaroscuro those graduations of shading which have hitherto been attributed to the photographer's left thumb over the lens.

We British have no monopoly of these newly-discovered gold-mines. A set of photographs of old Hamburg taken by Herr G. Koppmann in October 1883 recently changed hands at £800 and this despite the fact that they are said to be tinged with a slightly luminous blue haze. But Picasso had his blue period, so why not G. Koppmann and, come to think of it, why not me as well? Indeed I hope so, for this will bring added lustre to my studies of the launching of Q.E.2., the luminous blue haziness of which has hitherto been attributed to my over-prodigal use of an unfamiliar type of plastic glue.

Mrs. Cameron was a portraitist rather than a landscape artist and here she and I are on more competitive ground. I'm afraid, however, that I have little to set against the 23 studies of her pretty parlour-maid Mary Hillier, posing in various attitudes as a Madonna. All my collection can muster in this field is a characteristic though unfortunately footless portrait of my Grandmother's cook, Mrs. Worples. Mrs. Worples was a wizard with the skillet but she was, alas, no beauty. She could never, in one's wildest moments, have been described as Madonnabile. If the face of Helen of Troy launched 1000 ships, poor old Worpy's could hardly have got a coracle off the stocks. Nevertheless, Granny once caught her on Grandpa's lap after Sunday lunch and there was a monumental row. Would that my Box Brownie and I had been there to record the scene.

I suspect, however, that what really gives Mrs. Cameron's albums their extraordinary value is not so much their technical qualities as their straightforward biographical interest. Photographs of Browning and Tennyson, for instance, are not all that easy to come by and sharp-eyed students will be intrigued by her study of Palmerston which suggests that he must have been wearing somebody else's false teeth. Such, however, was her confidence in her work that when she sailed for Ceylon in 1875, Mrs. Cameron tipped the porters at Southampton with photographs of Carlyle.

Never mind; my albums have plenty to set against all this. Take, for instance, my study of HQ Troop bathing off the beach at Arromanches in June of 1944. That figure on the left is now a senior Diocesan Bishop, though you will note that his deportment in my photograph is shamefully unepiscopal. There is also a much-prized photo of the Author shaking hands with Winston Churchill during the 1951 Election campaign. Had there not been a button off my shirt at the time the picture would have been even more distinguished. Nevertheless, I'm perfectly prepared to try it on the porters at Southampton if I'm ever lucky enough to find one.

I think, however, that the *pièce de résistance* of my collection is a photograph of Einstein and myself taken in 1933 outside my rooms in Christ Church. That, I reckon, has got Mrs. Cameron licked into a cocked hat.

When Hitler threw Einstein out, Oxford very properly took him in. Einstein played the violin, though badly, and I performed equally badly on the cello. A chap on the next staircase named Widdrington, a rather serious chemist from Nuneaton, happened to play the piano and we used to foregather in his rooms after dinner and stumble through Schubert's *Trio in B flat Major opus 99*. Widdrington took this historic photo of his fellow musicians as we parted company one warm June evening and I got Einstein to autograph it for me. Unfortunately, in his muddle-headed, scientific way he inscribed it, "To my dear young friend Widdrington," and this sad misunderstanding has irked me ever since. However, there is this compensation. It will reduce my album's value for Wealth Tax.

On the other hand, the very first picture in my collection will undoubtedly bring it up again. Mrs. Cameron has nothing to touch it. Neither has Herr Koppmann. Nor, indeed, Mr. Annan. It is of myself at seven months old, lying on a fluffy white rug, beaming and totally nude.

Let's see what Sotheby's and Mr. Healey make of that.

"Dear Sirs, As a journalist I should be grateful if you would send me a review copy of the £945 edition of the collected works of Sir Winston Churchill; it is my intention to submit a review to the 'Megthorpe and District Bystander'. Thanking you in anticipation . . ."

PART 4
AND NOW
THE
GOOD NEWS

*"Cheer up, At least the country is no longer in
any doubt about the future."*

OIL
CHANGE

GRAHAM looks ahead to
the coming boom

*"You mean, Angus, that they canny get the oil tae the
refinery wi'oot piping it through oor wee croft?"*

*"I can't remember—did we ever have
a coal bonanza?"*

*"Still, it's nice to know that prosperity's just
around the corner."*

"Even a few thousand would keep us going till the stuff starts flowing ashore."

"By God, Carruthers, it might be like having an empire again."

'But not for ever, Miss Hewitt, will we be dependent on the whims of a few Arab sheiks.'

"Not only will it have a diving-board, Jon—it'll be heated."

IGNORANCE
IS BLISS

says cheerful Humphrey Lyttelton

I AM descended from a long line of pessimists. By the time it had reached my father's generation, gloom about practically every aspect of the present and future had become a family trait. My father even had a theme song, a glum little stanza which he used to sing in a sepulchral voice at family meals whenever the conversation lapsed. "Days and moments quickly flying . . . blend the living with the dead . . . soon will you and I be lying . . . each within his narrow bed." It didn't half liven up Sunday dinner.

It may be that my own invincible optimism derives from a youthful observation that few, if any, of his gloomy prognostications ever came to the sort of fulfilment that he expected. "I suppose you all realise," he announced one lunchtime in the late 'thirties, "that in five years time I shall be unable to move a muscle, with the possible exception of my eyeballs." He was in his middle fifties then, and despite a rheumatic disease which slowed him up a bit, he remained active enough to fall out of a tree at sixty-seven, get knocked off his bike by a careless motor-cyclist at seventy-two and be jolted off the top of a bus when not far short of eighty. Whenever we talked of doing something "next year" he would add in a voice of doom ". . . if there *is* a next year." Yet the years came and went without one, so far as I recollect, ever being cancelled.

Short of a recurrence of the Flood, the thing he dreaded most was a Run On The Pound. We had an Impending Financial Crisis in our house long before anyone else even began to suspect that there was something wrong, and I grew up in the belief that the fall of a couple of notches in the exchange rate of the pound brought the workhouse several streets nearer. Today I can look back with equanimity on a succession of runs on the pound which amount to nothing less than monetary diarrhoea, and the only time it ever had a noticeable affect on me was when a fee contracted in Deutschmarks for an engagement in Germany suddenly inflated behind my back.

126

Ignorance is at the base of much of my optimism. The fallacy in that popular literary device, the Fear of the Unknown, is that it is practically impossible to work up any fear of the unknown. When someone wags a finger in my face and threatens the worst economic disaster since the War, since the 'thirties, since the Fire of London, since the Battle of Hastings, since Alfred burnt the cakes, all I can do is return a placid, sheep-like stare because I don't know exactly what it is that I am supposed to worry about. Will it be like America in 1929, with me clamouring at the door of the bank unable to get at my overdraft and businessmen falling like autumn leaves from the upper storeys? If so, I take comfort in the statistic that Rudy Vallee, who played the saxophone and sang sloppy songs into a megaphone, forty-five years ago earned 7,500 dollars a week throughout the Depression.

I readily concede that I am no Rudy Vallee—I never did like his hairstyle, anyway—but history does suggest that there is a living to be made in music even in hard times, if one is prepared to make a few adjustments. It's a curious but clearly demonstrable fact that in periods of hardship and uncertainty, popular music turns its back on excitement and goes sentimental. The Wall Street Crash put paid to the hectic Jazz Age of the 'twenties, World War II brought to an end the frenetic Swing Era of the 'thirties, and I'll bet the severely de-valued but still buoyant shilling in my Post Office Savings Book that, if hard times really are just around the corner, they will halt in its tracks the Rock Epoch of the 'fifties, 'sixties and 'seventies. I give notice now that when it happens I am available, with an inexhaustible repertoire of soothing ballads, for Wakes, Winding-up Parties, Liquidation Balls and Bank-ruptcy Barbecues.

I'll bring my own megaphone, too, for Economic Collapse is not of course our only fashionable worry. If the adrenalin seems to be flowing too sluggishly we can always con-template the Energy Crisis. Here again, I appear to have manoeuvred myself unwittingly into a reasonably secure position. No member of my band needs to be plugged into the wall before he can utter a note, and the instruments we play are powered by nothing more sophisticated than human breath, over which neither Arab nor coal-miner nor electricity power-worker has any control. During one of the fuel crises of recent years, I had the ex-quisite experience of standing next to the bandstand when a Rock Band of some notoriety and indescribable volume was assailed by a power cut. One minute they stood there, legs arrogantly astride, guitars rampant, a ruthless master-race flaunting virility and soniferous violence. Then, at the throw of some distant switch, there was nothing there save the tuneless rattling of a lot of impotent curtain-wire, a bedlam of querulous oaths and the bewildered thrashing of a drummer whose incompetence was suddenly nakedly exposed. Until you have actually heard an electronically supercharged band instantaneously deprived of its life-blood, you have no conception of the blissful near-silence which will settle over the land when in the dying breath of radio an announcer gasps, "This is it, folks—all the electricity has run out!" I say "near silence" because I'll be there playing for my supper, as sure as my name's Rudy Vallee.

I suspect that I am not alone in viewing with calm if not pleasurable anticipation the threatened drop in our standard of living. I am one of those people who, for some reason probably connected with the time of day or night when they were born, seem to derive the maximum aggravation and the minimum benefit from the great blessings of our civilisation. If I use my tape-recorder, I end up wrestling with tape like Laocoon and the serpents. Judging by the lop-sided sound that emanates from my expensive stereophonic Sound Centre—the thing that used to be called a record-player—either a speaker is on the blink or I have gone deaf in one ear.

My colour television can only be said to give a satisfactory picture if, unknown to me, long-haired subversives have actually been at work painting the greens and fairways of Wentworth Golf Course bright red. Traffic lights with uncanny extra-sensory perception see me coming, blush and look away for five minutes. I can't even get any co-operation from that lady who gives the time on the telephone. Without fail she tells me that it's ". . .ty-nine and fifty seconds" so that, in a tearing hurry, I have to wait through all that pip routine. And I am expected to go cold with dread at the news that our standard of living has dropped back to where it was in 1972! I'm all for dropping back to 1948, if only to enable me to replace the faithful and indestructible Harris tweed sports jacket which I have worn since then and in which I propose to survive the economic Ice Age.

I am not, believe me, one of those euphoric crystal-gazers who believes that everything is going to go on improving for ever. I am a realist, as anyone must be who has reached the age of fifty-three and knows that his life is approaching the half-way mark. In 2021, the congratulatory telegram from King Charles III will be brought not, as I would like, by a boy on a red bicycle, but through a new handy table-top home-teleprinter in the wonder spray-on veneer that, even under a bright light, is indistinguishable from plastic.

I am pessimist enough to think that civilisation will march on, give or take the occasional hiccough. And optimist enough to think that I shall cope.